PRAISE I
REALIGNME
COLLEGE FOᴜ..ᴅ..ᴇᴇ ᴜ ᴜ.. ᴜ..ᴜ.. .

MW01515615

"Galloway provides a sensible way of restoring sanity to big-time college football at the same time that he outlines a championship playoff system. His reorganization of conferences and schedules would cut costs, boost revenues, and bring parity to a system that currently favors select universities. This would create the outcome uncertainty and excitement that characterizes the NCAA basketball tournament and show universities that Division I football could be sustainable. For anyone concerned with the future of college football, this book provides food for thought and a basis for constructive discussions."

Jay Coakley, Ph.D., Professor Emeritus
Sociology Department
University of Colorado, Colorado Springs
National Association for Sport and Physical Education
(NASPE) Hall of Fame

IT'S POSSIBLE!

REALIGNMENT AND PLAYOFFS – COLLEGE FOOTBALL'S OPPORTUNITY

SCOTT N. GALLOWAY

IPG

IT'S POSSIBLE!
REALIGNMENT AND PLAYOFFS –
COLLEGE FOOTBALL'S OPPORTUNITY

Published by:

Intermedia Publishing Group, Inc.

P.O. Box 2825

Peoria, Arizona 85380

www.intermediapub.com

ISBN   978-1-935529-94-1

Copyright © 2010 by Scott Galloway

Printed in the United States of America

No part of this publication may be reproduced, stored in a retrieval system, or transmitted in any form by any means – electronic, mechanical, digital photocopy, recording, or any other without the prior permission of the author.

All rights reserved solely by the author. The author guarantees all contents are original and do not infringe upon the legal rights of any other person or work. No part of this book may be reproduced in any form without the permission of the author. The views expressed in this book are not necessarily those of the publisher.

Dedicated to my son, David and daughter, Leah, who followed me into the coaching profession and to all coaches who choose "not be served, but to serve."

Never try to be better than anyone else, never cease trying to be the best that you can be.

Coach John Wooden

The pursuit of excellence is not an excuse for limiting the opportunities of others.

Robert McKelvain, Ph.D.

TABLE OF CONTENTS

PREFACE

Any change, even a change for the better, is always accompanied by drawbacks and discomforts.

Arnold Bennett

You may have picked up this book thinking it was about the silly conflict concerning which team deserves to be named national champion of college football, but, it is that and more. It is about how colleges across the nation conduct competition, and that is an important issue.

Competition, in its proper place, can be a very healthy, productive endeavor and has served this great nation well. It can also turn into a destructive force dividing people who would otherwise be united. This book is built on ideals that many Americans hold dear. Such as:

- The ideal of a level playing field where there is no external interference that affects the ability of the players to compete fairly

- The ideal that the game belongs to the players

and exists for their growth and development

- The ideal that games and championships should be won on the field, not in the boardrooms where conference commissioners strike exclusive million-dollar deals with bowl committees and television executives

- The ideal of the Golden Rule and that this respected concept be applied and used by college presidents, athletic directors and coaches as they cooperate with all participating college programs to structure fair competition which can instill the values and ethics that all Americans need to make this country great

- The ideal that competition is more about the pursuit of excellence and doing your best than just simply trying to be better than other people

I realize for some this may seem too idealistic, but ideals spur our passions and guide us in the way that we should go. With a well conceived plan we can put ideals to work. As Arnold Toynbee wrote:

Apathy can be overcome by enthusiasm, and enthusiasm can only be aroused by two things: first, an ideal, that takes the imagination by storm, and second, a definite intelligible plan for carrying that ideal into practice.

In this book you will read about a plan for establishing a

national championship playoff for college football. In the last few years, there has been much discussion about different plans for developing a playoff. My plan is one of the most radical and most comprehensive. It is "a definite intelligible plan" that Toynbee speaks of. I invite you to decide that for yourself.

How important is this issue? Michael Josephson, founder of the Josephson Institute, *charactercounts.org,* and author of *Pursuing Victory with Honor: The Ultimate Sportsmanship Tool Kit,* has some great things to say to leaders of sports leagues. In the preface of *Pursuing Victory with Honor*, Josephson discusses how sports values shape national values:

> The love of sports is so deeply embedded in our national consciousness that the values of millions of people—participants and spectators—are directly and dramatically affected by the values conveyed by organized sports. This places a significant social responsibility on those who influence sports—administrators, coaches, athletes and officials—to assure that athletic competition helps build the character and the ethics of participants and spectators. Many aspects of our American society are competitive, including our free enterprise system, and our views as to what is proper in the competitive pursuit of personal goals are influenced strongly by the dominant values of high profile athletic competition.

There is truth and wisdom in these words. After I developed the concept of a national championship playoff plan, it was Josephson's words and the words of others that spurred me on to share my ideas. Here are some more insightful words from Josephson:

> Those who have leadership opportunities and decision-making authority in shaping the values of organized sports have enormous power to uplift and improve the nature and character of our society. With this awesome power comes public responsibility.

If you are like me, you don't often read the preface of a book. Too many times, I just skip right to the first chapter. I am learning not to do that. I learned a great deal from Josephson's preface. Years ago, I learned how change takes place from the preface of a history textbook. The book was *The Ecumene: Story of Humanity*, written by William H. McNeil. The preface of that book started like this:

> This book is built around a simple idea: Men change their ways mainly because some kind of stranger has brought a new thing to their attention. The new thing may be frightening, it may be delightful; but whatever it is, it has the power to convince key persons in the community of the need to do things differently. . . . The central theme of human history, after all, is change—how men did new things in new ways, meeting new

situations as best they could.

How about that for an introduction to a history book! In 1981, I used the textbook as a teacher and have been carrying it around ever since. Little did I know I would use it to write a book myself. This book calls for change. If change takes place when "key persons in the community" become convinced that there is a better way to do things, I hope people will look seriously at this plan.

What you will read about in this book is a better way to conduct the competition between college football players. The current state of affairs in American college football is no longer acceptable. The chaos that exists today has evolved over time and is a result of leaders with good intentions doing what they thought best at that time. My objective is not to place blame, but rather propose a remedy. Over the last few years, we have heard many people complain about the Bowl Championship Series. Rather than complain about the problem, I thought I would try to come up with a solution.

There are going to be many plans designed to help bring about a national playoff for college football. This book will describe one. It is a dream that many will say is too far outside the box. It is my hope that readers will learn about this plan and decide for themselves what they believe to be good and right.

Some look at things that are, and ask why. I dream of things that never were and ask why not?

George Bernard Shaw

Christians are supposed not merely to endure change, nor even to profit by it, but to cause it.

Harry Emerson Fosdick

CHAPTER ONE
THE ISSUES WITH THE PRESENT SYSTEM

I cannot say whether things will get better if we change; what I can say is they must change if they are to get better.
Georg C. Lichtenberg

This is not a book about returning to the old days of college football. It is a book about improvement. When I coach, I tell players that there is no improvement without change. If you want to improve or get better, you must change. This is a book that calls for improvement through change in today's college football system.

Issue One: The system of determining a National Champion is based on opinion, not competition.

The college football national championship has historically been known as a "mythical" national championship. The World

Book Dictionary defines myth as, "a belief, opinion, or theory
that is not based on fact or reality." Dating back to the 1930s, a
panel of sportswriters selected a team to be crowned "national
champion" at the end of the regular season. Many years there
have been two teams named, one by the Associated Press and
one by United Press International. I doubt that the sportswriters
of the 1930s would have ever thought that their entertaining
little poll would evolve to someday be used to determine which
schools would be granted millions of dollars and which schools
would not. In fact, Alan J. Gould, the originator of the AP poll,
said, "Newspapers wanted material to fill space between games.
That's all I had in mind, something to keep the pot boiling."

Remember 1984? I do. I remember Brigham Young
University went undefeated and was crowned "National
Champions" of college football by the Associated Press. Did
BYU deserve to be called national champions? My friends who
were fans of the Southwest Conference believed that if BYU
had played in the tough SWC, they would not have been able
to go undefeated. I am sure my friends who were Southeastern
Conference fans felt the same, as did my friends who were Big 8
Conference fans. It has been said that the national championship
being awarded to Brigham Young in 1984 was the catalyst for
the eventual development of the Bowl Championship Series and
the division of the eleven conferences into two tiers comprised
of those schools that can and cannot get into the premier bowls.

The creation of the Bowl Championship Series was supposed
to give us a playoff for a national championship. Now, at the
end of the season two teams are selected to play in a "national

championship" bowl game. While the BCS system appears to be an improvement because it chooses two teams to play for a championship, the BCS system still relies on subjective opinion to decide which teams get to play for the championship. The BCS has been and will continue to be controversial as long as opinion determines who gets to play in the championship game.

Can you imagine a panel of sportswriters selecting the two NFL teams to play in the Super Bowl? Visualize, if you can, Little League baseball foregoing all the regional playoffs and the World Series in Williamsport, Pennsylvania to allow computers to pick two teams to play in a final championship game. Popular voting may work for elections and *American Idol*, but not for true athletic competition. Read what Craig Thompson, commissioner of the Mountain West Conference said before the Congressional Committee on Energy and Commerce, Subcommittee on Commerce, Trade and Consumer Protection:

> The current BCS system is based on a fundamentally flawed premise: that computers and pollsters can look at six or seven outstanding teams, all of whom have lost no more than one game (and few, if any, of whom have played each other), and decide which are the two best and should play in the national championship game. But, it is impossible to know which of those great teams are actually the best – unless they play each other. Computers don't know, pollsters don't know, and the BCS surely does not

know. Moreover, nearly half of the FBS teams
are eliminated from the national championship
even before the season begins. None of the 51
teams that play in Non-AQ Conferences can, for
all practical purposes, ever win a BCS national
championship given how the current system
is constituted. These teams are, in effect, done
before day one. A system that produces this result
is patently unfair.

Even the way the National Collegiate Athletic Association
conducts championships in football in the other divisions and
in other sports has too much subjectivity in the process. Can
you imagine the NFL, NBA or Major League Baseball assigning
a committee to select the teams that get to participate in
postseason playoffs? If other athletic organizations can conduct
championships without opinion polls, the fans that fund sports
can expect colleges to design a system that can, too.

**Issue Two: The structure of the conferences is outdated,
inconsistent and hinders growth and progress.**

There are 120 schools in the Football Bowl Subdivision
(FBS) of the NCAA. This division, formerly known as Division
I-A, has the peculiar tradition of playing exhibition games, known
as "bowl" games, after their regular season instead of having
a playoff to determine a national champion. There are three
other divisions in NCAA football; the Football Championship

Subdivision (formerly Division I-AA), Division II and Division III. These divisions play for a championship using a playoff.

The 120 schools of the FBS are divided into eleven conferences and three teams (University of Notre Dame, U.S. Military Academy and U.S. Naval Academy) compete as independents. The conferences have been formed as schools enter into agreements to compete against one another in athletic competition. The NCAA does not have input in the formation of these conferences, some of which were established before the NCAA itself. This lack of oversight has led to some inconsistencies. One conference, the Mid- American, has as many as thirteen schools. One conference, the Big East, has as few as eight schools. Some conferences are divided into two divisions and the teams don't play all the teams in the conference each season. Some conferences are not divided into divisions, and each team plays all the teams in its conference each season.

Conference membership determines the teams on a school's schedule and that schedule usually determines how many paying fans will attend the school's games. Money talks and money walks. Schools that have moved to the FBS since most of the conferences were formed can find it difficult to gain membership in the older, more established, and financially stronger conferences. Schools in these preferred conferences have no obligation to include these incoming schools. Only when schools extend invitations to other schools are there changes in the alignments. These alignments can change often if a conference believes an additional school would enhance its image or the money-making potential of the other member schools. Have you ever heard the expression, "dog-eat-dog world"?

I have lived in Texas, Oklahoma and Georgia. I have seen and understand the pride that Texans, Okies, and Georgians have in their state, their flagship universities and the football conferences they play in. Living in Atlanta, I have met Auburn, Tennessee, Florida and 'Bama fans. SEC fans are a lot like the old Southwest Conference fans I knew in my childhood. They believe the conference in which their favorite school plays is the best. It helps to ease the pain of defeat if you believe that every college team in the country would have lost if they had been required to play the same schedule your favorite team played. When I was a kid, SWC fans would not accept that Penn State could go undefeated if it had to play Texas or Arkansas.

Wikipedia defines ethnocentrism "as the tendency to look at the world primarily from the perspective of one's own culture. Ethnocentrism often entails the belief that one's own race or ethnic group is the most important and/or that some or all aspects of its culture are superior to those of other groups."

There is a "conferencecentrism" that is becoming increasingly prevalent. The lack of a national playoff fuels this kind of thinking. Conference television contracts contribute to this form of bias. Networks promote the conference they televise as the best or superior to all others. Pollsters cannot help but be influenced by the hype of television.

The feeling of superiority that these conference members and their fans possess seems to make them oblivious to the reality that the system is not just. Reporting on the huge ($2.25

billion, over fifteen years) television contract the SEC signed with ESPN, one headline on an Atlanta Journal Constitution blog read, "It's not a fair fight, and the SEC likes it that way." Wouldn't it be better if all the schools had an equal opportunity to play in a well-thought-of conference and play for a national championship?

Issue Three: The NCAA purpose does not match the goals of the conferences.

The NCAA, at ncaa.org states, "Our purpose is to govern competition in a fair, safe, equitable and sportsmanlike manner, and to integrate intercollegiate athletics into higher education so that the educational experience of the student-athlete is paramount." That seems sound to me. The issue I have is with the practice of the conferences. I emailed a college president about the idea of conference realignment to help facilitate a college football playoff. Here is part of his reply:

> . . . I have seen a number of proposals for a national championship developed over the years; however, yours is one of the more creative. As you noted, the structure of the current conferences is one of the most powerful forces within intercollegiate athletics. The six automatic qualifying conferences in the BCS have as their major goal the attraction of every dollar possible to their conferences.

Notice the conflict between the NCAA's purpose and

that of the automatic qualifying conferences of the BCS? We
have a problem. The NCAA says its purpose is to govern fair
competition. That seems to conflict with the goals of the BCS
conferences. It is doubtful the BCS conferences will voluntarily
submit to the NCAA. Conferencecentrism and the promotion of
certain conferences over others can undermine fair competition.

The importance of conference membership as a competitive
advantage in recruiting cannot be overstated. Often a school's
conference affiliation is more important to an eighteen-year-old
recruit than the school itself. More from the college president's
reply:

> I can assure you that there is no way in the
> world that they will disband, particularly the Big
> 10, PAC 10, SEC and the ACC. The Big 12 and the
> Big East are probably not as recalcitrant in terms
> of membership as are the other four. . . they [your
> ideas] simply are absolutely impractical given
> the intransigence of these conference members.
> I don't think it is a good use of your time to
> assume that you will find support within these
> conferences, or that you can generate support that
> will force these conferences to realign. They will
> come up with a way to generate the same level of
> financial support that you suggest, but try to keep
> most of it within their group of six conferences.

With words like "recalcitrant" and "intransigence," I had to
pull out the dictionary! This is what I learned. "Recalcitrant"
means resisting authority or control. "Intransigent" means

refusing to moderate a position, especially an extreme position; uncompromising. These conferences and the people charged with leading them have developed a powerful position in this system. It is improbable that they will be willing to submit to the authority of the NCAA and its stated mission. It is obvious that any change will be difficult. It may take an act of Congress!

State high school athletic associations know how to conduct a playoff for a championship. They do it every year. If the high schools can do it, don't you think the colleges should be able to figure it out?

Issue Four: The colleges have sold their game to third parties who make millions for staging postseason exhibition games called Bowl Games.

I have enjoyed many a New Year's Day bowl game. My first memory of such a game is the 1964 Cotton Bowl game between #1 Texas and #2 Navy. My dad loved to watch the bowl games, but he often expressed frustration that the contracts which bowl organizers signed with conferences kept great match-ups from occurring. I recall him being particularly irked in the 1964 season when undefeated Alabama was ranked #1 and undefeated Arkansas #2. Because of the bowl contracts, Alabama played in the 1965 Orange Bowl, and Arkansas, as the Southwest Conference champion, played in the Cotton Bowl. It would have been nice to see #1 vs. #2, but the bowl contracts would not allow it. Instead, SWC runner-up Texas played and beat Alabama in the Orange Bowl. Alabama stayed mythical national champions since at that time there was not a poll after the bowl games. Dad let his conference pride show by saying, "The national champs, Alabama, would have placed third in the Southwest Conference."

Bowl games were never meant to determine a national champion. Bowl games were designed to benefit the people who were staging the game. James Wagner of Pasadena, California got the brilliant idea that if a game was staged on January 1, people from the cold northeast would travel out to sunny California for the game and fall in love with the warm climate. It was hoped that these football fans would then buy some real estate and move west. The date and the location of the game were not set with the players' best interests in mind, but for making the most money. The concept of making money by hosting post-season exhibition games spread to New Orleans, Miami, El Paso and Dallas.

These post-season exhibition games really weren't even about rewarding the *best* teams with an extra game. The teams that would draw the most fans were the teams the bowl organizers were most interested in. The Cotton Bowl director once said, "I don't care if Houston is 9-0 or 99-0, they ain't going to the Cotton Bowl." My dad was particularly irked by that comment, but explained to me that the organizers of the Cotton Bowl did not want to see the UH fans drive in and out of Dallas without staying a few nights in the city's hotels. The third parties who organized these games were not interested in what was fair for the football teams or players. From their perspective, the bowl game was *their* enterprise and they could do what they wanted with it.

What once seemed to be a Win-Win for entrepreneurs and certain preferred conferences seems to be a big obstacle to running a fair and just athletic competition that would culminate in a national championship that is determined on the field. A national championship competition in which all schools could participate is not the priority of the third parties. In a December 18, 2008 article written for Yahoo Sports and entitled, "The Bowl Boondoggle," Dan Wetzel states:

> College football participates in one of the worst business arrangements imaginable. It outsources its most profitable and easily sold product—postseason football. . . . Bowl games, especially BCS games, are relics of the past; a billion-dollar-a-year industry existing for no apparent reason. It's been years since the NCAA needed to pay someone else to stage games . . . It's not how much money college football gets from the BCS bowls anyway. It's how much more it would get if it just staged the games itself . . . Adopting a playoff system would be vastly more profitable, but doing so would likely require the NCAA to run the event . . . The ticket money would stay in house, the TV cash would stay in house, just about everything, in fact, would stay in house. College football is so strangely corrupt it prefers the outhouse.

That was a scathing article and a gutsy one at that. It is well worth a read.

Wetzel provides detailed facts and figures regarding the millions of dollars that are being spent to stage these exhibition bowl games. When college football develops a true national playoff, there will be no need for third party business groups to convince fans to attend or tune in on TV.

Issue Five: The coaches themselves have been calling for change but have been ignored.

The coaches, those people closest to the players, know what is best for the game of football. Naturally, they are frustrated that play on the field is not determining a national championship. Since I have become engrossed in this issue, it is obvious to me that key people are not listening to the coaches. Here are some quotes from prominent coaches expressing their frustration with the current system.

> "To be frank with you, I don't know what the reasons are not to have a playoff. You can talk about missing class and all that kind of stuff, [yet] you see basketball go on forever. You have a lot of bogus excuses, but obviously the majority of the people who have the say don't want it. Not that I'm against what other people want to do, it's just that philosophically I think you ought to win on the field ... I have always been for a playoff."

> Coach Joe Paterno
> May 22, 2008
> ESPN.com

"We added a BCS game—for what in the world?—I understand we're avoiding lawsuits and making money. But let's take care of the players ... And you have presidents that for some reason look at it more as for the money than having a national championship on the field. They keep coming up with lame excuses about academics. Football players miss fewer classes than anybody . . . Presidents take the money and go spend it, but they don't worry about the business of making it better."

Coach Tommy Tuberville
October 4, 2006
ESPN.com

"I think we'll have a national playoff by 1998. I really do. But I hope it's for all colleges, not just a select few. It ought to be like NCAA basketball where everybody's got a chance."

Coach Fisher DeBerry
September 14, 1996
www.gazette.com

"I don't understand how the thing works, I don't really know. Maybe you guys will answer for it one of these days. Maybe you know and I don't. I'm sure you do . . . what is the criteria of the process? Is it to pick the team that has the best season, that has the season that you like the most and feel best about voting for? Or is it the best team at the end of the year, the team that would win a playoff system if you did have it?"

Coach Pete Carroll

www.collegenews.com

"It's beyond the fact of do we need a playoff, it's now, can we get one . . . It's an imperfect system, If you want a true national championship; the only way to do it is on the field."

Coach Urban Meyer

December 3, 2006

ESPN.com

"I hope one day we have a system where all the issues are decided on the field."

Coach Lloyd Carr

December 3, 2006

ESPN.com

Obviously there are some frustrated coaches who would like a playoff. The question will be how much are the people involved in the system willing to change the system?

I visited the American Football Coaches Association website expecting to see some statements about a coaches' movement to establish a playoff. I also stopped by the office in Waco. I studied the AFCA Code of Ethics and found the following statement from the document's preamble:

> Those who select football coaching must understand that the justification for football lies in its spiritual and physical values and that the game belongs, essentially, to the players.

How about that; coaches believe that the game belongs to the players! Has anyone asked the players what they want? I feel the coaches are sincere in their beliefs. If the game belongs to the players, then the system should reflect that!

Issue Six: The people in the system cannot seem to change the system.

In May of 2009, I watched with great interest the House of Representative's Energy and Commerce Committee hearing on the fairness of the BCS. Representative Joe Barton of Texas stated before the hearing that he was hoping to put pressure on college football to change voluntarily. One huge obstacle to changing the system is the way the Bowl Championship Series is governed. I learned from the hearing there are eight votes cast when the BCS governance board gets together. The six automatic qualifying conferences get one vote each. The University of Notre Dame gets one vote. The remaining vote goes to the fifty-one schools in the non-automatic qualifying conferences.

The weighted voting system may explain why the $190

million from the bowl games is so unevenly distributed. The six automatic qualifying conferences of the BCS receive up to 90 percent of the postseason income. It may also explain why teams from an automatic qualifying conference can get bowl invitations while finishing with 6-6 records like Oklahoma State and Alabama did in 2007. Troy University, on the other hand, of the non-automatic qualifying Sun Belt conference can finish 7-4 and not get to play in a bowl game. In 2007, Troy defeated Oklahoma State and Louisiana-Monroe on its way to seven wins. Louisiana-Monroe beat Alabama during the 2007 season. Troy was more deserving of the bowl money than Oklahoma State and Alabama. Troy also probably needed the money more. Troy is one of the fifty-one schools that collectively get to cast one vote when considering changes in the system.

During the congressional committee hearing, the explanation given for such an undemocratic voting process was that the schools in the automatic qualifying conferences have more tradition and are more popular than the schools of the non-qualifying conferences and therefore should have more say in the way the bowl system is run. It is this kind of thinking that created the system that so many believe needs to be changed. It is this kind of thinking that proves again that Albert Einstein was correct when he said, "We can't solve problems by using the same kind of thinking we used when we created them." College football appears to have been doing some stinking thinking and it wouldn't hurt for them to consider the thinking of those outside the system, like the many sports organizations that successfully conduct championships without polls or selection committees.

At the May 1, 2009 hearing, Rep. Bobby Rush of Illinois asked each of the guest panelists if they thought Congress should get involved in college football. Below is how Boise State Athletic Director, Gene Bleymaier answered:

> . . . Historically that change has only come with hearings like we are having today and unfortunately with the threat of lawsuit. It would be better for all served if the conferences could agree on a plan and a formula and approve it themselves, but because of the representation disparity that we have that is virtually impossible. The only way this is going to change is with help from the outside.

It sounds as if Mr. Bleymaier is asking for some help. I'm ready to help, are you?   Help could come in the form of some outside the box thinking, which is what this book will cover.

CHAPTER TWO
COLLEGES CAN LEARN FROM THE NATIONAL FOOTBALL LEAGUE

We live in a world in which things are accepted as normal without any thought as to whether they should be or whether there might be a better way. Too often we resign ourselves to accepting that things just are the way they are.

Coach Tony Dungy

Colin Cowherd hosts a sports talk show on ESPN radio, which airs weekday mornings in Atlanta on AM 680 "The Fan." In the weeks and months after developing the "true national championship" plan, I found myself listening to Colin almost daily. On more than one occasion, Cowherd spoke of how much he respects the National Football League for the way it runs professional football. Cowherd believes that the NFL is the best-managed sports league in the world. It must have been his perspective that made me compare how the NCAA governs college football versus the NFL's management of pro football. There is much to learn when we contrast the NFL with college football.

The NFL began in 1920 with eleven franchises or teams. Throughout its history, the league has grown and now boasts thirty-two teams. With the exception of the Green Bay Packers, all of the teams are owned by for profit companies. The Green Bay franchise was incorporated as a nonprofit corporation in 1922. It is impressive how much these for profit companies *cooperate* off the field so their teams can *compete* on the field.

When the NFL expands its league to include a new franchise, it does so after much thought and research. The Houston Texans are the latest team to be added to the NFL. The league office placed the Houston franchise in the South Division of the American Football Conference. The Texans' placement in the South Division ensured that they would host the Indianapolis Colts; a team that would help sell tickets for the new franchise. Another popular fan draw in the South Division would be the Tennessee Titans, the team that abandoned Houston and their Oiler name years earlier. Houston team owners did not have to fret about convincing other NFL teams to play them. It is a given that if you play in the NFL, the league office is going to issue a schedule and teams will play half their games on the road and half their games at home.

The new NFL franchise, Texans, opened their season by hosting the Dallas Cowboys. The Texans became the first NFL franchise in forty-one years to win their expansion debut when they defeated the Cowboys in Houston in front of 69,604 fans. I feel sure not all of the fans in the stadium were Texan fans, but there were many there to cheer on the Cowboys. What a great way to start play, by hosting your instant in-state rival and "America 's Team."

The Texans competed in their first season with an opportunity to earn post-season play by playing the NFL's finest teams. In the NFL, there are no bowl committees selecting the teams that get to play in the post-season. The winner of the AFC South Division is going to the NFL playoffs whether the sportswriters or so-called experts think the team deserves it or not.

Unlike professional teams, the 120 teams that play football in the NCAA's Football Bowl Subdivision are sponsored by colleges that are tax exempt, nonprofit corporations. You would think colleges that sponsor a sport for its educational value and receive millions of dollars of tax-deductible donations, would cooperate and collaborate better than the for profit professional teams. Think again.

The NCAA requires that schools applying for Football Bowl Subdivision (formerly Division I-A) status meet standards such as stadium size and a minimum number of scholarships and total sports offered. Once colleges meet those requirements and are accepted into the big time of college football, they can begin play. The NCAA does not place a school in a conference to compete in. Newcomers to the NCAA's top division are expected to find their own conference to compete in or they can remain "independent."

This NCAA practice has led to some very illogical conference alignments. For example, Louisiana Tech is in the

Western Athletic Conference with Hawaii and Boise State of Idaho. Other illogical alignments include Florida International with University of North Texas in the Sun Belt Conference and South Florida in the Big East with Syracuse University of New York. It is very rare for a school to gain membership into one of the powerful and financially secure BCS conferences that is geographically logical. Why? Unlike the National Football League, the NCAA has not concerned itself with conference alignments.

The NCAA also does not issue a schedule for the new member school to play. Schools are expected to schedule non-conference games by entering contractual agreements with other schools. Schools new to the "big time" most often have to play "guarantee (money) games" on the road at the more established program's home field. Games are also scheduled when two schools agree to play a home and home arrangement over a span of two seasons. It is very rare for a school new to the FBS to get to host a school from one of the six automatic qualifying conferences.

Troy University of Troy, Alabama began playing in the NCAA's Football Bowl Subdivision in 2001. Let's compare Troy's debut season with that of the Houston Texans. Troy opened its inaugural season in the FBS playing at Nebraska in front of 77,812 Cornhusker fans. I am sure the Cornhuskers paid the Trojans well to make the long trip to Lincoln.

In 2001, the Trojans also visited Miami, Mississippi State and Maryland, all members of automatic qualifying conferences in the BCS. Troy's first home game as a member of the FBS was against Nicholls State, a Division I-AA program. Not exactly the debut the Houston Texans had by hosting the Dallas Cowboys! A parallel debut for Troy would have been hosting either Auburn or the University of Alabama, two Southeastern Conference schools. Troy fans would have been very excited. The stadium would have been filled. The hotels and restaurants would have been filled. Both the southeast Alabama economy and the Troy athletic department would have prospered. To ensure that Troy would get to host Alabama or Auburn, the Trojans would have to gain entry into the SEC, which is done only by invitation from the member schools.

Many of the FBS schools new to the division have gone to great lengths and invested millions of dollars to eventually reach the point of playing at the NCAA's highest level. Some of these newcomers have made their way up from junior college status and have winning traditions achieved at each level. If the NFL can be structured for financial success for its expansion teams, you would think the NCAA could create a healthier financial environment for its newcomers.

The NFL is structured so that weaker teams can improve and succeed in the future. The NFL practices revenue sharing, believing that on the field competition is the life-blood for the league. Former NFL commissioner Pete Rozelle believed that comparable revenues would encourage on-field competition. Rozelle instituted a revenue-sharing scheme that gave each team roughly the same amount of money to spend on players. Rozelle felt that evenly talented rosters would help the growth of the NFL. Rozelle developed and shared a philosophy he called "League Think" that encouraged team owners to consider what was best for the whole league instead of focusing on their own teams. Ironically, the owners of the New York Football Giants, Jack and Wellington Mara, convinced the other owners that television revenue should be shared. At the time, the Giants were receiving four times the revenue that a smaller market like Green Bay was receiving. Such thinking allowed the teams to work collectively to strengthen the entire league. NFL owners invest their own money and then agree to share television revenue. That is impressive. Pro football is the most popular sport in the country with better TV ratings than college football.

The NFL allows the teams with the worst records to have the best opportunity to select the best college players for the future. The most successful teams or the teams with the best records are given the last picks in the draft of college players. In contrast, the most successful college football programs have a better chance to recruit the best high school players because they use the money they have gained from conference television contracts, season ticket sales and post-season bowl games to woo high school prospects to their campuses. In the NCAA, it seems the rich keep getting richer at the expense of the many college programs that are barely getting by.

It is interesting to me that the for profit companies that own the NFL franchises have set up a league where fairness and equal opportunity abounds. The major complaint about college athletics, which consists of universities operating as tax exempt nonprofits, is its unfairness. I realize that the NCAA is not the NFL, but perhaps for the good of college football, NCAA member schools could relinquish some of their autonomy to cooperate as professional football teams have. Maybe the goal of a true national championship playoff could provide the impetus for the NCAA front office to take more control. It seems obvious to me the laissez-faire approach of the past has not provided the healthy competition that is vital for players, coaches and fans alike.

CHAPTER THREE
HOW THE HIGH SCHOOLS DO IT

Progress is impossible without change, and those who cannot change their minds cannot change anything.

George Bernard Shaw

High School Athletic Associations across the country conduct state championships in football and other sports each year based on the belief that these championships contribute to the educational process. Colleges could learn something from these high school associations. The University Interscholastic League or UIL, which governs high school extra-curricular activities in the state of Texas, conducts state championships in multiple classifications for football. As a student-athlete in Texas, I understood that it was the responsibility of the UIL to divide the high schools into five classifications based on enrollment. After each school's classification was determined, the UIL then aligned the schools into competitive conferences, known as "districts" in Texas.

I grew up and played high school football in Mathis, a small farming town near Corpus Christi, Texas. Football was a big part of the Galloway family. My father, uncle and my older brother all played for Mathis. Dad would load us up in the station wagon when I was in elementary school, and we would drive miles to watch our hometown Pirates. It really did not matter if the Pirates were playing or not, we would find a game to watch. I can still remember that my grandfather drove us into Corpus Christi to watch Coles high school, the state champions of the Prairie View Interscholastic League, now defunct league for African-American schools.

My grandfather and father loved high school football and enjoyed telling us about different South Texas players. On the highways, we heard about Johnny Roland, who led his Miller High School team from Corpus Christi to a state championship before going on to star at Missouri, then the NFL's St. Louis Cardinals. Dad was instilling the values of working hard and being coachable when he would talk about Gene Upshaw and his brother, Marvin from nearby Robstown. Gene played at nearby Texas A&I before becoming at NFL hall of famer. Marvin went to school at Trinity before playing in the NFL. When our Pirates played at Bishop, we learned about its hometown great, Ronnie Bull who starred at Baylor before going on to the Chicago Bears. When we played at Ingleside, we heard about Coach Emory Bellard, the inventor of the infamous wishbone offense. Bellard's first coaching job was in Ingleside.

Most of my elementary school years, the 1960s, the Pirates struggled. Winning seasons were rare. Mathis was one of the poorest school districts in the state of Texas. When other school districts in the area, with money from oil, were building all-weather tracks and concrete football stadium bleachers, we were left with a dirt track and wooden bleachers. If we were in today's college athletic system, we would have definitely been labeled weak and not worthy to be in a BCS automatic qualifying conference.

For two straight seasons, in 1967 and 1968, our varsity team was winless, 0 and 20! I can still recall our varsity team getting beat 72-6 by George West High School. I was in junior high during those two seasons where my class won one game. We got clobbered also. Even though our team was not very good, football was still very important to the players and citizens of Mathis. That bears repeating, just because a school doesn't have a lot of winning tradition and huge fan following does not mean that the game is not important to the players. The game belongs to the players.

Life in Mathis in the late 1960s was somewhat troubling. There was racial tension that divided the community, so much that our little town was mentioned in both *Time* and *Newsweek* magazines. The population was made up of approximately 80 percent Mexican-Americans and 20 percent Anglos to use the terminology of the day, with a handful of African-Americans. Mathis was the talk of South Texas, but for the wrong reasons. It was a divided town and that division probably contributed to the losses of the football team.

Something had to change, and it did. Slowly and steadily

we put aside the differences that had divided us, and the Pirates began to win some games. My junior year we recorded a winning season. It seemed the whole town was looking forward to our senior season as most of our starters returned.

The UIL would realign the conferences, a.k.a. districts, in Texas every two years. It is done that often to ensure that schools are competing against schools with similar enrollment. UIL realignment took place before our senior season. Our team got the news that state powerhouse Refugio High would be moved into our district. Refugio was the preseason number 1 ranked team in the state! The Bobcats were legendary in South Texas. My sophomore year Refugio won the state title, its second trip to the finals in four years. If Refugio had been in the college world of athletics it definitely would have been a BCS privileged and preferred powerhouse! I remember people in town telling me, "too bad Refugio has moved into the district, y'all could have won the district title." Mathis had not won an outright district title in twenty-four years, when my dad played.

There was no avoiding Refugio. The Bobcats played in our district now and they were on our schedule. The UIL had spoken. We knew it, no protesting the decisions of the high school athletic association. It was the way it was done in high school, and all schools cooperated.

We worked very hard all spring and summer and dreamed of beating Refugio on its home field. On a foggy Friday night in October of 1972, the hard work paid off, we won 13 to 7. Our team earned the right to advance to the state playoffs by going undefeated against our district competition. Refugio stayed home that year. No writers voting on who gets to play in postseason bowl games; it was true competition. It's the playoffs. Players like it that way, no sitting around waiting to see if you get invited. It was simple. We knew what we had to do and did it. It is part of the educational process.

We won our first playoff game and advanced to the second round to play Freer High School, another oil rich school that had an indoor swimming pool. Mathis did not have a pool in town, much less an indoor one at the school. We had beaten the Buckaroos earlier in non-conference, so this was a rematch. Did the fans want to see a rematch? Who knows, the fans did not get to choose who was in the playoffs. Would a rematch be good for TV? Television was not a factor. Steve McMichael, Freer's sophomore nose-guard made for good TV later. He was a stud then and later a Super Bowl champion with the Chicago Bears. We won the rematch. A rematch can be a great learning experience for the players and coaches on both teams.

Improving to 12-0, we now were ranked second in the state. We learned again that rankings don't decide the outcome of the game, players do. Our playoff run and undefeated season ended the next week against Boling High who was led by a Colorado-bound and future Los Angeles Ram, Billy Waddy. Boling also had a Cinderella season. Boling started the season by losing its first three games, 0-3. Boling then righted the ship and stormed through the playoffs to the state championship.

Thankfully, the BCS or NCAA did not run high school

football in Texas in 1972. State high school athletic associations value sport for the life lessons the players learn. Our team learned that football rankings don't mean a thing. We also learned you can overcome the skeptics if you get a chance to prove yourself on the field. Several of my teammates went on to college ball and one, Shane Nelson, earned a scholarship as a walk-on at Blinn Jr. College. Shane eventually played at Baylor and then as an un-drafted free agent in the NFL with Buffalo and San Diego. Some fifteen years after high school, I met one of Shane's Baylor coaches, Corky Nelson. When I asked about Shane, Corky said that Shane had a "just watch me attitude" which meant if you tell Shane he couldn't do something, he would say "just watch me." I believe Shane learned that in the equal opportunity atmosphere that exists in high school football but is not as prevalent in college football.

The football team from Boling High learned a lot by losing its first three games. In college football today, three losses in your first three games would eliminate you from consideration by the expert pollsters. I spoke with then Boling assistant coach Bob Pyssen about the 0-3 start. He told me they got off to a rocky start because they were trying to give a player a chance to develop at quarterback. Those three losses taught them they had to adapt. Moving the great Billy Waddy from running back to quarterback was the decision that turned their season around. The Boling players learned the importance of believing in themselves when others did not. Participating in sports helps teach some valuable lessons for high school players, college players and professional players. It seems that college administrators minimize the value of those lessons for the players.

In 1972, the UIL had aligned all the state's schools of Mathis' classification into thirty-two districts. Roughly, there were 240 schools playing in our classification. Every team in the state started the season playing for a chance to advance to the playoffs and be crowned state champions. There were no privileged BCS automatic qualifying conferences in high school, *all* thirty-two district champions earned their way into the playoffs. Were there some districts or conferences considered stronger than others? Sure! Mathis and Refugio were both ranked in the state's top ten that season, but the polls did not decide who advanced to the playoffs, the players did. Was it somehow unfair that two of the state's best teams had to play in the same district, with the loser being eliminated from postseason play? It was understood by the seventeen-year olds playing that sometimes it happens that way and you learn to live with it. The coaches and players knew that in order to have a state championship playoff, it had to be that way.

If high school athletic associations can govern state championships without the use of polls, it can be done at the college level too. The foundation of the high school competition is the alignment of the schools into conferences by an objective, impartial governing body. This makes the competition impartial and fair for all the schools. As a college student in Athletic Administration, I was fortunate to study the University Interscholastic League Constitution. I also was privileged to hear the Director of the UIL, Dr. Bailey Marshall, explain the process of aligning the schools in Texas into geographically based-conferences. Dr. Marshall stressed the importance of forming the conferences objectively, using geographic proximity as a basis. The Encarta Dictionary's definition of "objectively" is "without bias; without being influenced by personal feelings." The alignment of teams into thirty-two districts or conferences was critical for creating a playoff bracket. Having an odd number of conferences would lead to some subjective seeding or placement of teams.

Athletes that truly want to compete want a chance to prove themselves on the field. There is a greater sense of self-responsibility when an athlete or team competes without sportswriter rankings, selection committees and retired coaches attempting to judge which team is best. Do you agree? High school athletic associations seem to understand this better than the college system that has acted as though there is some sort of gift for judging teams and deciding who would win a match-up.

Notice the University Interscholastic League of Texas "Statement of Purpose" below, taken from its website. It is a statement of the values that most of us hold dear.

Statement of Purpose[1]

The University Interscholastic League believes:

- participation in extracurricular activities motivates students to place a high priority on attending school and making better grades.

---

[1]   "UIL: About the UIL." *University Interscholastic League*. Web. 06 May 2010. <http://www.uil.utexas.edu/about.html#purpose>.

- that most students enjoy the pursuit of excellence and seek opportunities to test themselves against their own accomplishments and the accomplishments of others,

- that such opportunities are best provided through properly conducted and equitably administered competitive activities,

- that the classroom is enriched by the flow of student energy into the more intensified arena of competition and back into the classroom.

Therefore, we reaffirm that students are the focus of our endeavor and deserve an opportunity to:

- refine physical and mental skills,

- nurture self-realization and build self-confidence,

- feel a sense of pride and dignity,

- experience teamwork and develop a sense of fair play,

- develop the ability to lead and the willingness to follow,

- foster self-discipline and perseverance,

- appreciate that rules, consistently applied, create order and discipline,

- learn to accept graciously the decisions of judges and officials,

- affirm self-worth in times of disappointment as well as adulation,

- cultivate lifetime skills,

- complement their classwork with practice and performance,

- have fun,

- experience the joy of achieving their potential in a wholesome environment, and

- discover that ultimately the true meaning of winning is doing one's best.

High schools throughout this nation have united behind similar sets of values. The commitment to shared values allows for collective action, for the good of the students, sport and education.

Is a high school playoff that leads to a state championship game popular with fans? The state of Texas has been using a playoff without polls or selection committees for decades. High schools throughout the state are subject to conference realignment every two years. The result is a well run athletic competition that teaches student-athletes life lessons about fair play and sportsmanship. Attendance at some Texas high school playoff games compares favorably with some of the new bowl games that have been created in recent years.

Texas High School Football Playoff Games[2]

Attendance is not an official statistic kept at Texas high school football playoff games, so state records are incomplete.

Attendance for these ten games is among the highest on record in Texas history:

Attendance	Game	Site	Year
49,953	Plano vs. Port Neches-Groves	Texas Stadium	1977*
46,339	Southlake Carroll vs. Euless Trinity	Texas Stadium	2006
45,790	Highland Park vs. Waco	Cotton Bowl	1945*
45,000	Houston Washington vs. Galveston	Rice Stadium	1968
45,000	Dallas Adams vs. Richardson	Cotton Bowl	1967
39,102	Garland vs. Katy	Astrodome	1999*
39,102	Stephenville vs. Port Neches-Groves	Astrodome	1999*
38,570	Port Neches-Groves vs. Houston Kashmere	Astrodome	1977
38,374	Plano vs. Highland Park	Texas Stadium	1980
38,000	Odessa vs. San Antonio Jefferson	Memorial Stadium	1946
36,000	Fort Bend Willowridge vs. Houston Yates	Rice Stadium	1988

*state championship game

---

2   "History," *Texas High School Football*. Web. 06 May 2010.
<http://txprepsfootball.com/Recordbook.htm>.

CHAPTER FOUR
RECRUITING AND THE CONSPIRACY TO KEEP IN-STATE COLLEGES OUT OF OUR LEAGUE

He has honor if he holds himself to an ideal of conduct though it is inconvenient, unprofitable, or dangerous to do so.

Walter Lippmann

The colleges in the preferred and privileged automatic qualifying BCS conferences have a recruiting advantage. The extra money the schools receive from being a member of an automatic qualifying conference helps to maintain that advantage. Money is only part of the story. The other great advantage is the public perception that these schools are bigger and better than the schools that are members of the non-automatic qualifying conferences. It is one thing to gain advantage on the field it is another to have an advantage gained by simply being in a preferred and privileged conference.

The driving force in college athletics is recruiting, recruiting, recruiting. So image is everything. I learned that lesson first hand when I transitioned from high school coaching to college coaching.

As a high school coach, I worked very hard at teaching sound fundamentals and training the athletes that I had to become good players. A high school coach is expected to teach the players and hope some really talented players come along. In other words, most people are happy with a high school coach if his team is well coached but not as talented as the competition.

In contrast, a college coach is responsible for getting the talented athletes to his school. That is why a coach's ability to recruit is often seen as more important than his ability to teach. Often times a college coach is considered a failure and will be fired if his players are well coached but not as talented as the competition.

Therefore recruiting dominates thinking in college athletics. Just about every decision made in an athletic department, is made considering how recruiting will be impacted. The success of a college's recruiting effort is dependent on how a college and its competitors are perceived by the sixteen and seventeen year -olds living in the state or region. It helps to be the flagship university in your state and the only program playing in the Football Bowl Subdivision (Division I-A). Nebraska, Boston College, Wisconsin and Minnesota enjoy this position. These schools do not have a lot of competition in recruiting in-state football players. LSU, Arkansas and Colorado enjoy the position of being the only universities in their state in the top tier automatic qualifying BCS conferences.

In the state of Alabama, the University of Alabama has had to contend with Auburn in recruiting the state's best talent. The rivalry between these two schools is intense. Auburn fans claim that for years Alabama refused to play at Auburn. So the game was held in Birmingham, much closer to Tuscaloosa than to Auburn. While other conference teams had to play at Auburn, Alabama did not. Finally, on December 2, 1989, Alabama played at Auburn and the Tigers won just as the Crimson Tide were afraid they would. The game was a boom to the town of Auburn bringing thousands to the local economy.

It has also been said that Auburn and Alabama conspired to hinder the University of Alabama at Birmingham's attempt to field a football team. I assume Auburn and Alabama felt more competition in the in-state recruiting wars would only make it more difficult to win in the Southeastern Conference. UA-Birmingham, which fielded its first team in 1991, is a member of Conference USA, not a top-tier automatic qualifying BCS conference. Also, creating more competition for recruits in Alabama has been the rise of Troy University. Troy has made its way up the NCAA division ladder, becoming a FBS program and Sun Belt Conference member in 2001. Thanks to these two schools moving into the NCAA's FBS division, there are more football scholarships available for young athletes, because moving up a division means increasing the number of scholarships for football.

Alabama has not played UAB or Troy. Auburn has played UAB one time in 1996, but has not played Troy. Often coaches, in the situations like Alabama and Auburn find themselves, are afraid that they have everything to lose and nothing to gain by playing the in-state schools that play in other leagues. Currently, Auburn and Alabama have what I call the "they are not even in the same league" recruiting advantage over the other in-state schools. To the general public, Troy and UAB are the new kids on the block and are not considered in "the same league" with Alabama or Auburn. Auburn and Alabama do not want to risk the loss of that perception, so therefore they avoid playing these schools. They certainly would not want all the schools to be in the same conference and therefore be forced to play *at* Troy and *at* UAB. Historically, the NCAA has done little to organize or align the conferences, so therefore schools can keep in-state competitors out of their conference and avoid playing them.

When I was growing up in Texas in the 1960s, The University of Texas won three mythical national championships in '63, '69 and '70. That is, the "expert" pollsters voted that the Longhorns were the best team in the nation. In order to do that, the Longhorns had to get by a strong Arkansas program. Texas and Arkansas dominated the SWC in the 1950s and '60s. That dominance ended when the Southwest Conference expanded to include the University of Houston in 1976. The powerhouse Cougar program won the conference championship in its very first year and three championships in the first four years of league play.

We can learn something from looking at the history of the Houston program. In the 1960s, the Cougars enjoyed some success as an independent being ranked in the AP Top Twenty, for five straight years. After moving to the SWC, the Cougars achieved their highest rankings ever, No. 4 in 1976 and No. 5 in 1979. So what changed? It is my belief that a great deal of Houston's success nationally came as a result of their membership in the Southwest Conference. Being included in the SWC for the first time in 1976 put the Cougars in the media spotlight in the state of Texas that influenced pollsters and gave them a greater opportunity to recruit the state's top football prospects.

Many high school athletes often dream of playing for the flagship school in their state. If that school does not want them, then the next best thing for those players is to play in "the same league" for another school. Arkansas' roster included many Texans back when they competed against Texas in the Southwest Conference. The Houston area was a hotbed of talent. With the Cougars now in the same conference with the Longhorns of Texas, UH became a viable option. The city of Houston was more attractive to eighteen year olds than College Station, Waco or Lubbock. Even Arkansas probably lost some recruiting battles to Houston.

How much did Houston's inclusion in the respected SWC impact recruiting for the University of Texas? It is hard to say, but in the twenty years before the Cougars entered the SWC, Texas won eleven conference titles and three mythical national titles. In the twenty years that Houston enjoyed membership in the SWC, the Longhorns won five SWC titles and zero national titles.

When the Big 8 Conference sought to expand by taking four SWC schools, it caught many Texans by surprise when Houston was not included with Texas, Texas A&M and Texas Tech. Rumor has it that Baylor graduate and then Texas governor Ann Richards pulled some strings for her alma mater. My guess is that A&M, Texas or Tech preferred that Baylor enter the Big XII. They probably felt they could have more success recruiting against Baylor than against Houston.

Since their exclusion from the Big XII in 1996, the Houston Cougars have joined the newly formed Conference USA, which has included East Carolina, Cincinnati and Louisville. They have not finished a single season ranked in the top twenty. While a member of the SWC, the Cougars finished the season ranked in the top twenty 6 times, the last time being 1990.

So what has happened? Of course there is not one single factor, but I believe the major factor is that the Cougars are no longer "in the same league" with the University of Texas and that makes a huge difference in recruiting in-state high school athletes. The Houston media is not going to give Conference USA the same exposure as it would the Big XII conference. So high school players will choose Texas A&M or Texas Tech over the Cougars. There was a time when it wasn't so.

Since I have decided to write about this subject, I have shared the story of the Houston Cougars with many of my friends in Texas. I asked them the following question: "If the University of Houston was in the Big XII conference, could the Cougars have signed Vince Young instead of Texas?" It has been a unanimous, "yes that's very possible." Remember, Texas did not win a national championship while the Houston Cougars were "in the same league" with the Longhorns and I doubt they could have done it if Vince Young had signed with the Cougars.

I am not alone in thinking that conference membership impacts recruiting. Former Ohio State and Minnesota Viking running back, Robert Smith, does excellent work as a college football analyst for ESPN. A fellow analyst asked Smith, "How would Boise State do if it was competing in the PAC 10?" Smith, without hesitation, said that if Boise State competed in the PAC 10, they would be able to recruit better players and certainly would be able to compete in the conference. Smith knows what so many average fans do not know and that is that much of college athletic success is about conference reputation.

ESPN Analyst and former Notre Dame Head Coach, Bob Davies had some interesting comments about the University of Arkansas' recruiting and conference affiliation. During a game with Texas A&M, Davies stated that Arkansas would be a better fit in the Big XII conference, hinting their recruiting base should be the Dallas-Fort Worth area. As a member of the Southwest Conference, the Razorback's many appearances in Texas helped them load up on Texas high school recruits. Davies understands the critical factors that influence recruiting.

That speaks for the power and importance of conference membership!   Conference membership is a huge factor in recruiting. It is far too important for the NCAA office to ignore. The gamesmanship that goes on in scheduling and self-formation of conferences warrants the NCAA's involvement.

CHAPTER FIVE
CURRENT CONFERENCE ALIGNMENTS

The dogmas of the quiet past are inadequate to the stormy present. The occasion is piled high with difficulty, and we must rise with the occasion. As our case is new, so we must think anew and act anew.

Abraham Lincoln

College and universities have been forming conferences for over one hundred years. You might say the current alignment of the conferences is a result of Evolution. The alignments could use some Intelligent Design. Unlike professional leagues and many state high school associations, the NCAA does not have any say over conference alignment. In my opinion, this is the most obvious weakness of college athletics.

History shows that these voluntary athletic conferences are in a constant state of change, some increase in size, while others decrease. Conferences realign when its members feel it is in their best interest. Since postseason football play and the money that is attached to postseason play is based on opinion polls it has become extremely important to play in what is perceived to be a strong conference. If writers and other pollsters have a low opinion of a school's conference, their votes will reflect that.

In most sports leagues, amateur or professional, winning your conference will advance you to postseason play and it doesn't matter if your conference is highly thought of or not. College athletics is different, using opinion polls and selection committees to pick postseason participants in some sports. Being in the right conference can make or break a school's athletic department. Many a critic has told me that the conferences will never realign because there is too much money being made by the schools in the preferred conferences.

2009 Conference Alignments of
Football Bowl Subdivision Schools

Automatic Qualifying Bowl Championship Series
Conferences

The conferences known commonly as the "BCS conferences" are those conferences that have contracts with the traditional bowl games and are able to get the big money that goes to the BCS bowl games. If indeed, college football is a two-tier system as Representative Neil Abercrombie of Hawaii suggests, this is the top tier.

Atlantic Coast Conference

School	Location	Enrollment	Joined ACC
Boston College	Chestnut Hill, Massachusetts	9,019	2005
Clemson	Clemson, South Carolina	13,959	1953
Duke	Durham, North Carolina	6,259	1953
Florida State	Tallahassee, Florida	31,058	1991
Georgia Tech	Atlanta, Georgia	12,360	1979
Maryland	College Park, Maryland	24,876	1953
Miami	Coral Gables, Florida	10,132	2004
North Carolina	Chapel Hill, North Carolina	16,278	1953
N. Carolina State	Raleigh, North Carolina	22,879	1953
Virginia	Charlottesville, Virginia	13,387	1953
Virginia Tech	Blacksburg, Virginia	21,937	2004
Wake Forest	Winston-Salem, N.Carolina	4,231	1953

The Atlantic Coast Conference has expanded recently by adding Boston College, Florida State, Miami and Virginia Tech. Those schools abandoned the Big East conference. Creating a two division super conference allows for the conference to make money from a conference championship game between the winners of the two divisions. While that might make sense for football competition, it hardly seems sound financially for Miami to send its non-revenue sports teams to Boston.

It is 1,261 miles from Miami, Florida to Boston, Massachusetts. During the 2009 volleyball season, the University of Miami team of the Atlantic Coast Conference, traveled to Boston to play fellow Atlantic Coast Conference member, Boston College.

Boston College returned the favor by traveling those same 1,261 to play the Hurricanes in Miami. Those volleyball matches were part of the conference schedule. These two schools played "home and home" conference games in men's and women's basketball. The teams also competed in men's tennis, women's tennis, women's soccer and baseball, with either BC or Miami making the long trek. Each team travels 2,400 miles a contest and I counted a total of ten contests for a total of 24,000 miles traveled for volleyball, basketball, tennis, soccer and baseball competition. The increased travel demands for the non-revenue sports do not make sense academically either.

Big East Conference

Institution	Location	Enrollment	Year Joined
Cincinnati	Cincinnati, Ohio	36,518	2005
Connecticut	Storrs, Connecticut	28,411	1979
Louisville	Louisville, Kentucky	21,841	2005
Pittsburgh	Pittsburgh, Pennsylvania	32,105	1982
Rutgers	New Brunswick, New Jersey	34,696	1995
South Florida	Tampa, Florida	40,261	2005
Syracuse	Syracuse, New York	18,247	1979
West Virginia	Morgantown, West Virginia	28,113	1995

Big East Conference schools
Participating in sports other than football

DePaul	Chicago, Illinois	23,570	2005
Georgetown	Washington, D.C.	13,612	1979
Marquette	Milwaukee, Wisconsin	11,510	2005
Notre Dame	South Bend, Indiana	11,415	1995
Providence	Providence, Rhode Island	3,648	1979
St. John's	Queens, New York	19,813	1979
Seton Hall	South Orange, New Jersey	9,700	1979
Villanova	Villanova, Pennsylvania	9,500	1980

Originally, this conference was organized as a basketball conference with many schools like Georgetown, Providence, St. John's, Seton Hall and Villanova not playing D-I football. After losing Miami, Boston College and Florida State to the ACC, former Conference USA members, Louisville, Cincinnati and South Florida were added. One of the said requirements for the BCS designation has been tradition, history and popularity. Some of these schools don't meet that subjective criteria as well as Brigham Young, Houston and Utah, but they were in the right place at the right time and now receive preferential treatment through BCS monies. Like the Atlantic Coast Conference, the recent expansion of the Big East has resulted in some illogical travel situations for some schools. The addition of Marquette of Milwaukee, Wisconsin, DePaul University of Chicago and Notre Dame of South Bend, Indiana (for sports other than football) has added to the travel budgets of these athletic departments in the Big East.

Big Ten Conference

Institution	Location	Enrollment	Joined
Illinois	Urbana /Champaign, Illinois	42,728	1896
Indiana	Bloomington, Indiana	43,247	1900
Iowa	Iowa City, Iowa	30,409	1900
Michigan	Ann Arbor, Michigan	40,025	1896
Michigan State	East Lansing, Michigan	45,520	1953
Minnesota	Minn./Saint Paul, Minnesota	51,194	1896
Northwestern	Evanston, Illinois	13,407	1896
Ohio State	Columbus, Ohio	52,568	1912
Penn State	University Park, PA	42,914	1990
Purdue	West Lafayette, Indiana	39,333	1896
Wisconsin	Madison, Wisconsin	41,466	1896

This conference, which has a contract with the Rose Bowl is older than the NCAA itself. The conference expanded to eleven teams when Penn State was added in 1990. The expansion of the Big 10 seemed to set off a chain reaction that led the Southeastern and Big 8 conference to expand to twelve teams. Michigan, Ohio State and Penn State historically have the highest attendance numbers in the nation. This is the oldest of the major conferences. The Big 10 has been benefitting from bowl money longer than the other conferences. The conference also has its own television network which broadcasts a vast array of sports on cable and or satellite. In 2009, the Big 10 announced that it would be expanding to twelve schools. Speculation is that the new school will be Notre Dame. I have also heard the University of Texas is attractive with all the television sets in the Lone Star state.

Big XII Conference

Institution	Location	Enrollment	Joined
Iowa State	Ames, Iowa	26,160	1996
Kansas State	Manhattan, Kansas	23,332	1996
Colorado	Boulder, Colorado	28,624	1996
Kansas	Lawrence, Kansas	29,260	1996
Missouri	Columbia, Missouri	28,405	1996
Nebraska	Lincoln, Nebraska	22,973	1996
Baylor	Waco, Texas	13,886	1996
Oklahoma State	Stillwater, Oklahoma	23,819	1996
Texas A&M	Coll. Station, Texas	46,540	1996
Texas Tech	Lubbock, Texas	28,260	1996
Oklahoma	Norman, Oklahoma	29,721	1996
Texas	Austin, Texas	49,696	1996

The Big XII was established in 1996 when the schools of the Big 8 raided the Southwest Conference of Texas, Texas A&M, Texas Tech and Baylor, leaving SMU, TCU, Rice and Houston scrambling for a conference home. Houston and SMU have never been the same. Oklahoma, Oklahoma State, Kansas and Missouri have flourished with recruits that might not have left the Lone Star state without the breakup of the SWC.

One of the storied rivalries in all of college football, the OU-Nebraska matchup was damaged with the creation of this super-conference. Since OU and Nebraska are in different divisions, the conference schedule does not have them playing annually, only every few years. I think this development has hurt

Nebraska's national exposure and hurt their revenue. If you will look at the recent history of Nebraska football you will notice a decline that coincides with the creation of this conference. Oklahoma still has a nationally televised game with Texas and in 2008, games with Big XII South division opponents Texas Tech and Oklahoma State were among the most watched in the nation. The Big XII does not distribute TV revenue evenly among all conference members. The South Division has been thriving with more revenue being directed to Oklahoma, Texas and their division opponents.

Pacific 10 Conference

Institution	Location	Enrollment	Joined
Arizona	Tucson, Arizona	37,036	1978
Arizona State	Tempe, Arizona	64,394	1978
California	Berkeley, California	33,000	1959
Oregon	Eugene, Oregon	20,333	1964
Oregon State	Corvallis, Oregon	19,276	1964
Stanford	Palo Alto, California	14,654	1959
UCLA	Los Angeles, California	38,000	1959
Southern California	Los Angeles, California	32,160	1959
Washington	Seattle, Washington	42,708	1959
Washington State	Pullman, Washington	23,121	1962

The Pacific 8 became the Pac 10 in 1978 when Arizona and Arizona State were invited to join. Brigham Young and Utah were also considered during expansion, but the nod went to the

Arizona schools. One sports anchor I know said that the Pacific 8 schools preferred the Arizona schools over the Utah schools because the advantage of the two- year Mormon mission that Mormon athletes enjoy. I would like to know how many more high school players from California were added to the rosters of the Arizona schools after their inclusion with USC and UCLA. I have to believe that more California schoolboys left their home state to play in Arizona.

Southeastern Conference

Institution	Location	Enrollment*	Joined
Florida	Gainesville, Florida	51,913	1932
Georgia	Athens, Georgia	33,831	1932
Kentucky	Lexington, Kentucky	27,209	1932
South Carolina	Columbia, South Carolina	27,065	1991
Tennessee	Knoxville, Tennessee	26,400	1932
Vanderbilt	Nashville, Tennessee	11,607	1932
Alabama	Tuscaloosa, Alabama	25,580	1932
Arkansas	Fayetteville, Arkansas	18,647	1991
Auburn	Auburn, Alabama	24,137	1932
Louisiana State	Baton Rouge, Louisiana	33,587	1932
Mississippi	Oxford, Mississippi	17,323	1932
Mississippi State	Starkville, Mississippi	17,032	1932

The SEC has long been considered one of the top, if not the top conference in college football. Even as strong and stable as this conference has been, its members have changed over the years. At one time, Tulane and Georgia Tech were in the SEC. In an effort to attract more TV viewers, Texas was invited to join when Arkansas broke away from the Southwest Conference. When Texas turned down the invitation, South Carolina was added.

Independents

Institution	Location	Enrollment
United States Military Academy	West Point, New York	4,000
United States Naval Academy	Annapolis, Maryland	4,400
Notre Dame	South Bend, Indiana	11,603

Fifty years ago, in 1959, there were seventeen schools playing as independents without a conference. Two of the most storied programs in college football history, Notre Dame and Penn State both played as independents until 1990 when Penn State joined the Big 10. I don't recall any NFL, NBA or MLB teams playing as independents. Most sports leagues are made up of teams that have a spirit of interdependence rather than independence.

The maps below illustrate some of the chaos that has been created with conference alignment and realignment. The first map shows land encompassed by the "automatic qualifying" conferences. As you can see there is overlapping with four of the six "BCS" conferences. It was virtually impossible to show all eleven FBS conferences on one United States map because of the overlapping, so I have included another map showing the vast amount of land traveled by "non-automatic qualifying" conference schools.

Map of the "Automatic Qualifying" Conferences

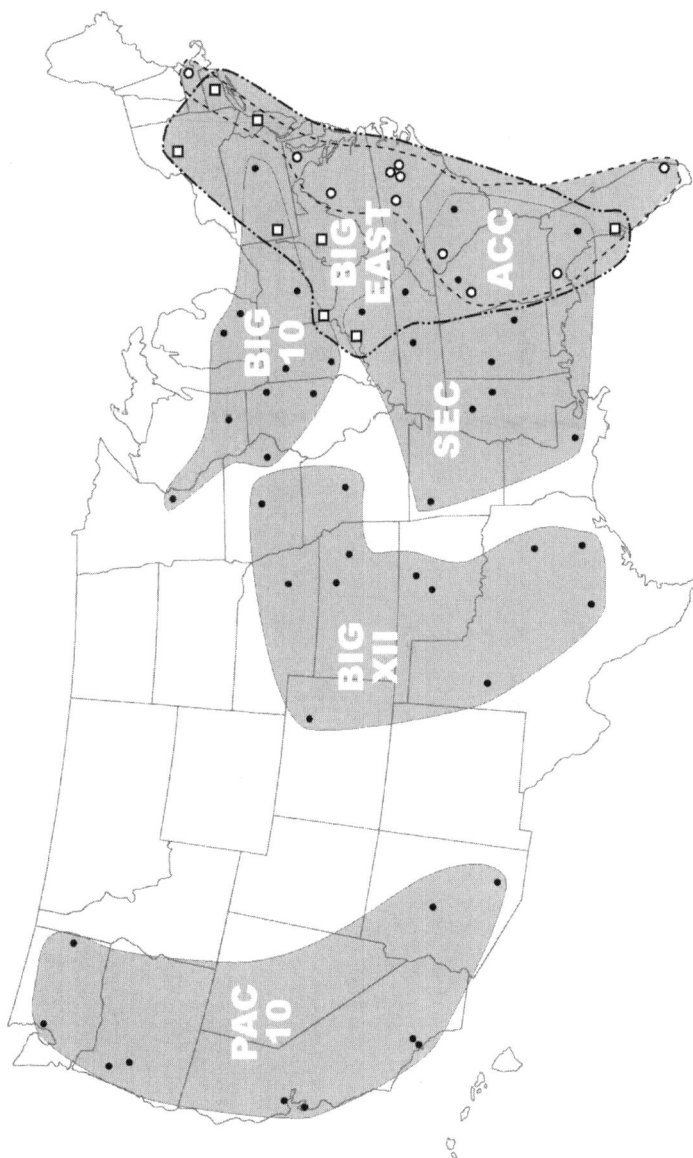

Map of "Non-Automatic Qualifying" Conferences

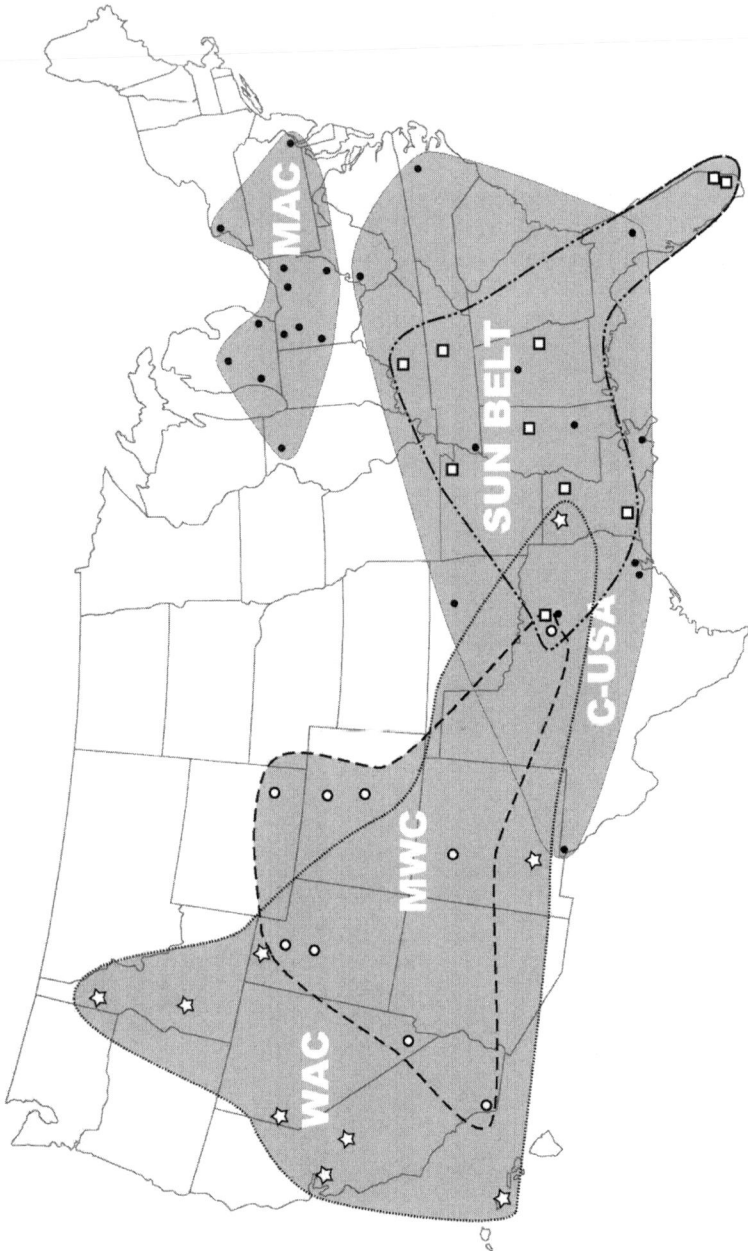

"Non-Automatic Qualifying" BCS Conferences

The conferences listed below are commonly known as non-BCS because the champion of these conferences do not have an automatic tie-in to the high paying BCS bowl games, the Fiesta, Orange, Rose and Sugar. The Bowl Championship Series leaders would rather you call them "non-AQ" conferences for non-automatic qualifier. The history of the bowl games has played a part in this awkward distinction.

As you look at this list, you may recognize that some of these schools, Houston and SMU were once aligned with schools in the automatic qualifying BCS conferences. You will also note that these schools are not the "small schools." Some of these schools have been playing football many, many years but have been at a geographic disadvantage, located away from the media limelight. Some schools like Boise State and Troy were successful in other divisions of college football before making the difficult transition to "D-IA" or the Football Bowl Subdivision. With the success of some of these schools in recent years, BCS critics have hammered the system and called for reform.

Conference USA

Institution	Location	Enrollment	Joined
Houston	Houston, Texas	35,180	1995
Rice	Houston, Texas	4,835	2005
Southern Methodist	Dallas, Texas	10,901	2005
Texas at El Paso	El Paso, Texas	20,154	2005

Tulane	New Orleans, Louisiana	13,214	1995
Tulsa	Tulsa, Oklahoma	4,174	2005
UAB	Birmingham, Alabama	17,600	1995
Central Florida	Orlando, Florida	48,497	2005
East Carolina	Greenville, North Carolina	25,990	1997
Marshall	Huntington, West Virginia	16,400	2005
Memphis	Memphis, Tennessee	20,668	1995
Southern Mississippi	Hattiesburg, Mississippi	15,050	1995

Conference USA has been a revolving door since its creation in 1996. Some of the original members have jumped to the Big East Conference, one of the preferred BCS conferences. Texas-El Paso was once part of the Western Athletic Conference as was Rice, SMU and Tulsa. The distance from Huntington, West Virginia to El Paso, Texas is 1,430 miles, which is quite a trek for the Marshall student-athletes playing volleyball and softball in the 2009-2010 academic year. I am all for travel and seeing the country, but it has to be hard on students, not to mention the budget.

Mid-America Conference

Institution	Location	Enrollment	Year Joined
Akron	Akron, Ohio	23,000	1992
Bowling Green	Bowling Green, Ohio	23,338	1952
Buffalo	Buffalo, New York	27,220	1999
Kent State	Kent, Ohio	34,056	1951
Miami	Oxford, Ohio	20,126	1948
Ohio	Athens, Ohio	28,804	1947
Ball State	Muncie, Indiana	20,113	1973

Central Michigan	Mount Pleasant, Michigan	26,788	1972
Eastern Michigan	Ypsilanti, Michigan	22,827	1972
Northern Illinois	DeKalb, Illinois	24,998	1997
Toledo	Toledo, Ohio	21,270	1951
Western Michigan	Kalamazoo, Michigan	24,433	1948
Temple	Philadelphia, PA	34,218	2007

Every school in the MAC listed a higher enrollment than one third of Southeastern Conference schools. For many, there is a perception that the schools playing in the preferred BCS conferences are bigger schools with better academics. That is a perception the automatic qualifying schools enjoy and would most likely want to maintain. However, the MAC boasts the highest graduation rate for football players among all the conferences. This conference is made up of schools from many of the same states that make up the Big 10 conference.

Mountain West Conference

Institution	Location	Enrollment	YearJoined
Air Force Academy	Colorado Springs, Colorado	4,000	1999
Brigham Young	Provo, Utah	32,400	1999
Colorado State	Fort Collins, Colorado	26,418	1999
New Mexico	Albuquerque, New Mexico	24,092	1999
San Diego State	San Diego, California	34,500	1999
Texas Christian	Fort Worth, Texas	8,749	2005
Nevada, Las Vegas	Las Vegas, Nevada	31,000	1999
Utah	Salt Lake City, Utah	29,192	1999
Wyoming	Laramie, Wyoming	13,162	1999

The Mountain West Conference has many of the original WAC members that decided they did not like the two-division super conference concept and split in 1999. TCU has been added in recent years. Utah has finished undefeated two times in 2004 and 2008 and their win over Alabama in the Sugar Bowl added to the anti-BCS sentiment. This conference can argue that many of their teams have better history and tradition than some schools in the BCS conferences.

Sun Belt Conference

Institution	Location	Enrollment	Joined
Arkansas State	Jonesboro, Arkansas	16,494	2001
Florida Atlantic	Boca Raton, Florida	26,000	2001
Florida International	Miami, Florida	39,500	2001
Louisiana-Lafayette	Lafayette, Louisiana	18,079	2001
Louisiana-Monroe	Monroe, Louisiana	8,140	2006
Middle Tennessee	Murfreesboro, Tennessee	22,554	2001
North Texas	Denton, Texas	32,181	2001
Troy	Troy, Alabama	27,148	2001
Western Kentucky	Bowling Green, Kentucky	18,391	2009

The Sun Belt conference features many schools that are new to the Football Bowl Subdivision designation. These schools face an uphill battle trying to get the media attention while playing in the shadow of the Southeastern Conference. As mentioned earlier Louisiana-Monroe traveled to Alabama and came away with a win in 2007. Troy had a better record than Alabama and a win over Louisiana-Monroe in 2007. Alabama got money for playing in a bowl game; Troy did not play in a bowl. At the time only the Sun Belt conference champion was guaranteed a bowl game.

Western Athletic Conference

Institution	Location	Enrollment	Joined
Boise State	Boise, Idaho	19,500	2001
Fresno State	Fresno, California	21,000	1992
Hawaii	Honolulu, Hawaii	20,549	1979
Idaho	Moscow, Idaho	13,000	2005
Louisiana Tech	Ruston, Louisiana	11,710	2001
Nevada	Reno, Nevada	15,588	2000
New Mexico State	Las Cruces, NM	16,415	2005
San José State	San José, California	28,932	1996
Utah State	Logan, Utah	23,128	2005

The WAC has been through much realignment since the "super conference trend" started in the early 1990s. Many of the original WAC members are now in the Mountain West. Boise State has made a big splash rising from junior college status in the 1940s to a victory over Oklahoma in the Fiesta Bowl. Also, notable is Louisiana Tech being aligned with these far west schools. It doesn't make much sense.

It is 1,613 miles "as the crow flies" from Moscow, Idaho, the home of the University of Idaho of the Western Athletic

Conference, to Ruston, Louisiana, where Louisiana Tech, also a Western Athletic Conference member, is located. That is about 3,200 miles round trip. Those schools competed in home and home contests in volleyball, men's basketball and women's basketball. At least one team made the long trip in football, women's soccer and softball.

The aforementioned conference travel demands are not the most extreme. The University of Hawaii is also a member of the Western Athletic Conference. The distance between Moscow, Idaho and Hawaii is 2,880 miles. It is a whopping 4,034 miles to Hawaii from Ruston, Louisiana. Where is the logic in these schools being in the same conference, playing "home and home" contests in baseball, volleyball or anything else for that matter? This situation is a result of each school trying to find a conference in which to compete and no strong authority to realign conferences as the nation grows.

CHAPTER SIX

THE PROPOSED REALIGNED CONFERENCES

Tradition simply means that we need to end what began well and continue what is worth continuing

Jose Bergamin

Below are the 120 schools placed in realigned conferences. This realignment is necessary to create a fair and equitable system for all of the schools playing in the Football Bowl Subdivision. The proposed alignment was done with objectivity, using geographic location as the basis for alignment. Also, much care was taken to align schools from the same state together. The reasoning is that schools in the same state are generally recruiting students and student-athletes that are residents of that state. This will also prevent some schools from refusing to play in-state schools. Local and regional media will be able to focus on a single conference and not be forced to choose to cover one conference over another. The media attention a conference and a school receive is vital to that school's image and recruiting.

You will notice that eight of the realigned conferences consist of seven schools and the other eight conferences consist of eight schools. With conferences this size, each school will play every conference school each season. With a conference championship and a berth in a national championship playoff at stake, it is important that every team play each other. I believe the super-conferences that require interdivisional crossover games do not give teams equal opportunity because some teams play a more difficult schedule than others.

Conference 1

Institution	Location	Enrollment
1.Boise State	Boise, Idaho	19,500
2.Idaho	Moscow, Idaho	13,000
3.Nevada	Reno, Nevada	15,588
4.Nevada-Las Vegas	Las Vegas, Nevada	31,000
5.Oregon	Eugene, Oregon	20,339
6.Oregon State	Corvallis, Oregon	19,276
7.Washington	Seattle, Washington	42,708
8.Washington State	Pullman, Washington	23,121

This conference unites four states that each has two schools playing in the FBS. The in-state rivalries will be interesting and each school could continue to play some of the historic rivalries from previous conference affiliation, Pac-10, Mountain West and WAC. Nevada-Las Vegas did not start playing football until 1968. Nevada began playing in D-IA in 1992, Boise State and Idaho in 1996.

Conference 2

Institution	Location	Enrollment
1.California	Berkeley, California	33,000
2.Fresno State	Fresno, California	21,000
3.Hawaii	Honolulu, Hawaii	20,549
4.San Diego State	San Diego, California	34,500
5.San Jose State	San Jose, California	28,932
6.Southern California	Los Angeles, California	32,160
7.Stanford	Palo Alto, California	14,654
8.UCLA	Los Angeles, California	38,000

This is almost an all California conference, but it is the logical place for Hawaii. Travel to Hawaii will be more economical for the California schools than for Louisiana Tech! No offense to Louisiana Tech or New Mexico State, but I would bet hosting USC will draw more attendance for the Fresno State and San Jose home games. Programs like San Diego State, Fresno State and San Jose State will gain more credibility with California schoolboys if they are in the same conference with USC, Stanford, California and UCLA.

Conference 3

Institution	Location	Enrollment
1.Arizona	Tucson, Arizona	37,036
2.Arizona State	Tempe, Arizona	64,394
3.Brigham Young	Provo, Utah	32,400
4.New Mexico	Albuquerque, NM	24,092

5.New Mexico State	Las Cruces, NM	16,415
6.Utah	Salt Lake City, Utah	29,192
7.Utah State	Logan, Utah	23,128

This conference looks interesting to mc, because Arizona and Arizona State return to play against old WAC foes. Can Utah and Brigham Young continue their recent success if they have to play Arizona and Arizona State? The great thing about the proposed system is that the players are going to decide things on the field.

Conference 4

Institution	Location	Enrollment
1.Air Force	Colorado Springs, Colorado	4,000
2.Colorado	Boulder, Colorado	28,624
3.Colorado State	Fort Collins, Colorado	26,418
4.Iowa	Iowa City, Iowa	30,409
5.Iowa State	Ames, Iowa	26,160
6.Nebraska	Lincoln, Nebraska	22,973
7.Wyoming	Laramie, Wyoming	13,162

There are four states represented here with some natural rivalries from within the states of Colorado and Iowa. Colorado and Nebraska would retain their rivalry from their Big 8 and Big XII history. Iowa meeting on a regular basis against Nebraska could get interesting as well.

Conference 5

Institution	Location	Enrollment
1.Kansas	Lawrence, Kansas	29,260
2.Kansas State	Manhattan, Kansas	23,332
3.North Texas	Denton, Texas	32,181
4.Oklahoma	Norman, Oklahoma	29,721
5.Oklahoma State	Stillwater, Oklahoma	23,819
6.SMU	Dallas, Texas	10,901
7.Texas Christian	Fort Worth, Texas	8,749
8.Tulsa	Tulsa, Oklahoma	4,174

This conference features some Big XII rivals with some Texas schools that have been on the outside looking in on the BCS scene. With a total of ten Texas schools, it was impossible to keep them all together, while maintaining a consistent number of schools (seven or eight) throughout the nation. The Texas schools were divided geographically with the three schools closest to Oklahoma and Kansas placed in this conference. One of the great things about this conference is that schools like Tulsa, TCU, SMU and North Texas will get to host Oklahoma. That should give those schools some clout in recruiting circles. The Oklahoma and Kansas schools will appreciate the opportunity to make appearances in talent rich Texas.

Conference 6

Institution	Location	Enrollment
1.Baylor	Waco, Texas	13,886
2.Houston	Houston, Texas	35,180
3.Rice	Houston, Texas	4,835
4.Texas	Austin, Texas	49,696
5.Texas A&M	College Station, Texas	46,540
6.Texas-El Paso	El Paso, Texas	20,154
7.Texas Tech	Lubbock, Texas	28,260

If this looks familiar, there is a reason. Six of these schools competed against each other in the now defunct Southwest Conference. The new kid on the block will be Texas-El Paso. When the University of Texas played at UTEP in 2008, the Sun Bowl stadium had its first regular season sellout. Economists estimated the Longhorn's appearance in El Paso meant 3.8 million dollars to the local economy.

Conference 7

Institution	Location	Enrollment
1.Arkansas	Fayetteville, Arkansas	18,647
2.Arkansas State	Jonesboro, Arkansas	16,494
3.LSU	Baton Rouge, Louisiana	33,587
4.Louisiana Tech	Ruston, Louisiana	11,710
5.Louisiana-Lafayette	Lafayette, Louisiana	18,079
6.Louisiana-Monroe	Monroe, Louisiana	8,140
7.Missouri	Columbia, Missouri	28,405
8.Tulane	New Orleans, Louisiana	13,214

Can you believe that the state of Louisiana has five schools playing in the FBS? Only one of those schools has been in an automatic qualifying BCS conference; LSU. I spent the night in Ruston recently and imagined what the atmosphere would be like if LSU came to town to play Louisiana Tech. Arkansas would be forced to play Arkansas State in Jonesboro. I could not find any record of that ever happening. The decision to include Missouri here was not easy. Missouri could also be placed in Conference 8 with the Illinois and Indiana schools.

Conference 8

Institution	Location	Enrollment
1.Ball State	Muncie, Indiana	20,113
2.Illinois	Urbana/Champaign, Illinois	42,728
3.Indiana	Bloomington, Indiana	43,247
4.Northern Illinois	DeKalb, Illinois	24,998
5.Northwestern	Evanston, Illinois	13,407
6.Notre Dame	South Bend, Indiana	11,603
7.Purdue	West Lafayette, Indiana	39,333

The biggest surprise of this conference would be the inclusion of Notre Dame in a conference! The Fighting Irish have always been an independent in football. They have seen fit to have their basketball program added to the Big East conference when it was in their best interest. All schools will have to be willing to submit to the authority of the NCAA in order to facilitate a national championship that everyone has equal chance to play for.

Conference 9

Institution	Location	Enrollment
1.Central Michigan	Mount Pleasant, Michigan	26,788
2.Eastern Michigan	Ypsilanti, Michigan	22,827
3.Michigan	Ann Arbor, Michigan	40,025
4.Michigan State	East Lansing, Michigan	45,520
5.Minnesota	Minn./St. Paul, Minnesota	51,194
6.Western Michigan	Kalamazoo, Michigan	24,433
7.Wisconsin	Madison, Wisconsin	41,466

This conference would include four Big 10 schools and three Michigan schools that have competed in the Mid-America Conference. I just have to believe that Central, Eastern and Western Michigan fans will love the opportunity to see their team host the Big Blue of Michigan. How would Michigan feel about playing home and home with these schools? For those panicking over Ohio State not being included with Michigan, there is always a non-conference date available to continue that rivalry.

Conference 10

Institution	Location	Enrollment
1.Akron	Akron, Ohio	23,000
2.Bowling Green	Bowling Green, Ohio	23,338
3.Cincinnati	Cincinnati, Ohio	36,518
4.Kent State	Kent, Ohio	34,056
5.Miami of Ohio	Oxford, Ohio	20,126

6.Ohio	Athens, Ohio	28,804
7.Ohio State	Columbus, Ohio	52,568
8.Toledo	Toledo, Ohio	21,270

The state of Ohio loves its football as evidenced by the fact that eight schools in the state play in the FBS division. Would you look at the enrollments of those schools? Many may say that there is Ohio State and then the rest, but Cincinnati has made some noise recently. Once again, the question will be how does realignment impact recruiting? I have to believe some Ohio schoolboys now leave the state to play in the Big 10 against the Buckeyes when they can't play for the Buckeyes. I predict those schoolboys will stay in Ohio and that will strengthen all of the programs.

Conference 11

Institution	Location	Enrollment
1.Kentucky	Lexington, Kentucky	27,209
2.Louisville	Louisville, Kentucky	21,841
3.Marshall	Huntington, West Virginia	16,400
4.Maryland	College Park, Maryland	24,876
5.Navy	Annapolis, Maryland	4,400
6.Rutgers	New Brunswick, New Jersey	34,696
7.West Virginia	Morgantown, West Virginia	28,113
8.Western Kentucky	Bowling Green, Kentucky	18,391

The two teams listed at the top are sure to have a great in-state rivalry in this conference. This conference is made up of teams from four states currently in the Big East, ACC, SEC, Conference USA and the Sun Belt. West Virginia, Rutgers and Louisville have spent time in the top ten in recent years. It is worth noting that Western Kentucky has played in the Division II championship game and the Division I-AA championship game before transitioning to the FBS. I would say they have earned the opportunity to move into this division.

Conference 12

Institution	Location	Enrollment
1.Army	West Point, New York	4,000
2.Boston College	Chestnut Hill, MA	9,019
3.Buffalo	Buffalo, New York	27,220
4.Connecticut	Storrs, Connecticut	28,411
5.Penn State	University Park, PA	42,914
6.Pittsburgh	Pittsburgh, Pennsylvania	32,105
7.Syracuse	Syracuse, New York	18,247
8.Temple	Philadelphia, Pennsylvania	34,218

This conference promises some real interesting match ups. Buffalo and UCONN have been making strides since moving to the FBS division at the turn of the century. A move into a conference with traditional power Penn State will help their rise. Pittsburgh and Penn State promises to be a great rivalry.

Conference 13

Institution	Location	Enrollment
1.Clemson	Clemson, South Carolina	13,959
2.Georgia	Athens, Georgia	33,831
3.Georgia Tech	Atlanta, Georgia	12,360
4.Memphis	Memphis, Tennessee	20,668
5.Middle Tennessee	Murfreesboro, Tennessee	22,554
6.South Carolina	Columbia, South Carolina	27,065
7.Tennessee	Knoxville, Tennessee	26,400
8.Vanderbilt	Nashville, Tennessee	11,607

This conference unites some natural in-state rivals. For years, Tennessee tried to avoid playing Memphis. In this alignment that would be impossible. Today, Georgia plays Georgia Tech and Clemson plays South Carolina. Middle Tennessee fans will jump with joy when they get to host the Volunteers which would help finance their move into the FBS.

Conference 14

Institution	Location	Enrollment
1.Duke	Durham, North Carolina	6,259
2.East Carolina	Greenville, North Carolina	25,900
3.North Carolina	Chapel Hill, North Carolina	16,278
4.North Carolina State	Raleigh, North Carolina	22,879
5.Virginia	Charlottesville, Virginia	13,387
6.Virginia Tech	Blacksburg, Virginia	21,937
7.Wake Forest	Winston-Salem, NC	4,231

This conference looks a lot like a division of the ACC with the big exception being the East Carolina Pirates crashing the party. Interestingly, the highest enrollment of this group is East Carolina's. All of these schools are capable of winning this league.

Conference 15

Institution	Location	Enrollment
Alabama	Tuscaloosa, Alabama	25,580
UAB	Birmingham, Alabama	17,600
Auburn	Auburn, Alabama	24,137
Mississippi	Oxford, Mississippi	17,323
Mississippi State	Starkville, Mississippi	17,032
Southern Mississippi	Hattiesburg, Mississippi	15,050
Troy	Troy, Alabama	27,148

In my research of the history of the conferences, I learned that Alabama has never played Troy or Alabama-Birmingham. In their first season, in D-IA, Troy defeated Mississippi State. I have to believe that towns like Troy and Hattiesburg will benefit greatly from hosting in-state schools on Saturdays during the football season.

Conference 16

Institution	Location	Enrollment
1.Central Florida	Orlando, Florida	48,497
2.Florida	Gainesville, Florida	51,913
3.Florida Atlantic	Boca Raton, Florida	26,000
4.Florida International	Miami, Florida	39,500
5.Florida State	Tallahassee, Florida	31,058
6.Miami	Coral Gables, Florida	10,132
7.South Florida	Tampa, Florida	40,261

Would you look at the enrollments of these Florida schools? The state of Florida produces some of the nation's best high school prospects. Most of those prospects will stay in the state to play in this conference. Attendance should be outstanding at any of the stadiums in Florida. South Florida has been playing football since 1997, Florida Atlantic since 2001 and Florida International since 2002. These new programs should flourish when they get to host Florida State, Florida and Miami.

Map of Proposed Realigned Conferences

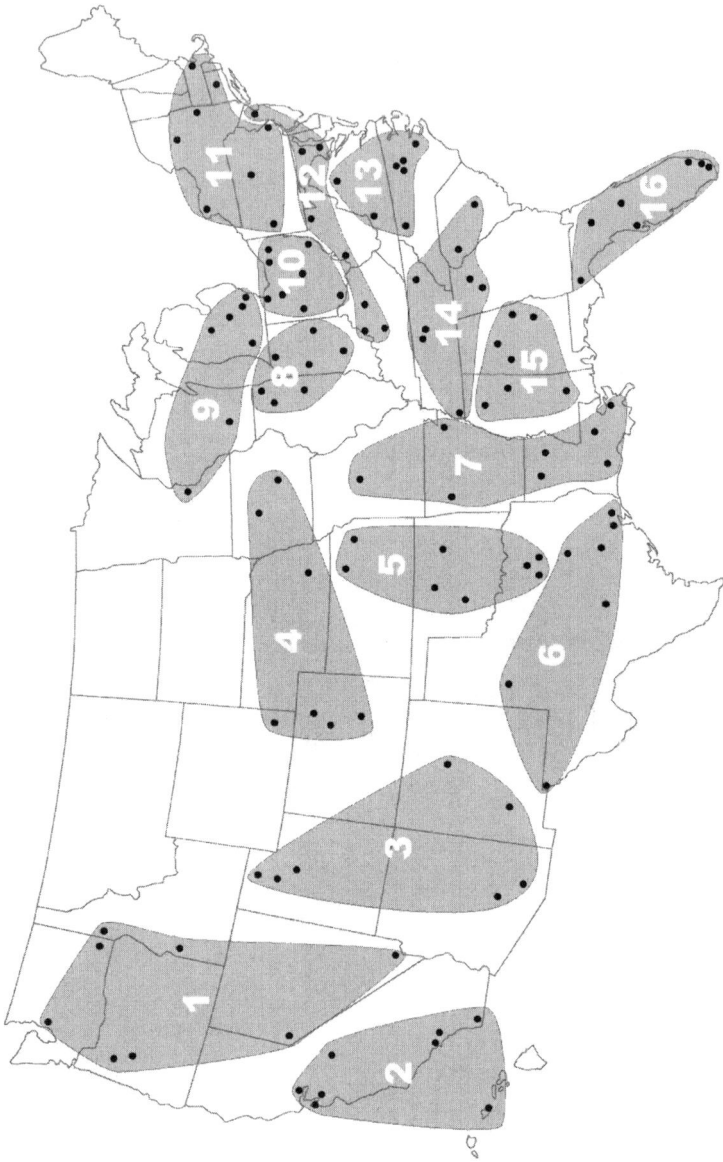

Conference Realignment would help "green" college athletics.

I confess to you that I am not the most "Green" individual that you will meet, but it seems to me that the current conference alignments aren't very green either. Conservation is just another reason to consider realigning the conferences. Another reason would be the loss of class time for all the athletes making those excessively long trips.

In my proposed conference realignment, Miami would be aligned with FBS schools in Florida and only be required to play "home and home" games within its conference. With the proposed realignment, Boston College's most distant conference foe would be the University of Pittsburgh, 480 miles away. Louisiana Tech's most distant foe after realignment could be Missouri, 444 miles away. That is 400 not 4,000. Of course, any school that is in a conference with Hawaii will have travel expense challenges, but better California schools than Louisiana.

Having shared this realignment proposal with a number of people I know many think they will not be able to get used to the changes, but changes have been taking place in the conferences since their inception. A major plus of sixteen conferences with either seven or eight member schools is that schools new to the Football Bowl Subdivision or Division I-A can be added more easily. As I have mentioned before, in order for this plan to be implemented, the colleges are going to have give up some of their autonomy and submit to the NCAA as authority.

CHAPTER SEVEN

SCHEDULING IN THE NEW REALIGNED SYSTEM

Society, community, family are all conserving institutions. They try to maintain stability, and to prevent, or at least to slow down, change. But the organization of the post-capitalist society of organizations is a destabilizer. Because its function is to put knowledge to work – on tools, processes, and products; on work; on knowledge itself – it must be organized for constant change.

Peter F. Drucker

In the past, getting to the mythical championship game meant making sure your non-conference schedule was such that you racked up wins against weaker opponents, sometimes opponents from other divisions. Season ticket holders are often times disappointed by the non-conference home schedule. In the newly realigned conference system, fans will be the beneficiaries of some great match-ups. Schools will be more willing to schedule some powerhouse programs for their non-conference schedule. One of my responsibilities as a coach at both the college and high school level was scheduling non-conference games. The conference schedule at both the high school and college level was decided by the conference and agreed upon by member schools. Working up a non-conference schedule involved a lot of phone calls to negotiate getting schools to travel so we could have home games.

In high school, most scheduling is done through reciprocal agreements. "If you will agree to come play us this season, we agree to come play you next season." That seemed fair to me, you know, the Golden Rule, "treat people the way you would want to be treated if you were in their situation." Such reciprocity is rare in college scheduling! I was not aware of that, but I learned quickly.

A different version of the Golden Rule exists when scheduling at the college level. It is, "He who has the gold, rules." Money, sometimes hundreds of thousands of dollars is exchanged when many non-conference games are scheduled. Most of the moneyed powerhouse programs pay big money to have the "lower tiered" programs come play at the home field of the traditional power. The powerhouse programs do not want to travel to play a road game so rather than make reciprocal agreements to play "home and home" they buy their opponents with what is known as a "guarantee" game.

It seems to me that if Oklahoma invites the University of North Texas to play at Norman, the Sooners should be willing to play

UNT in Denton, Texas. I realize there may be situations where a school like UNT might want to just take OU's money rather than play the Sooners in Denton. People have their reasons, but if I am coaching at UNT, I would love the opportunity to excite the student body and fans with an upset win on my home field. In recent years, UNT has played at OU, at Texas and at LSU most likely out of necessity to raise funds. If any of those powerhouse programs showed up in Denton, it was only to recruit some of Denton's fine schoolboy prospects, not to play UNT.

Many people that have seen my playoff plan have expressed disappointment at the thought that historic rivalries like Ohio State-Michigan or Georgia-Florida would end with conference realignment. My comment to them is that it would not be necessary to end these rivalries, if the schools in question wanted to schedule a non-conference game. There are some great, historic rivalries that exist without the two schools being conference opponents, USC-Notre Dame and Florida-Florida State come to mind. Until 1996, the Texas-Oklahoma rivalry was a non-conference contest.

So what would your favorite team's schedule look like in a new realigned conference? Let's take a look at some hypothetical situations. You may be surprised.

2009 Florida Schedule
Sept 5   Charleston Southern
Sept 12   Troy
Sept 19   Tennessee*

Sept 26   at Kentucky*

Oct 10   at LSU*

Oct 17   Arkansas*

Oct 24   at Mississippi State*

Oct 31   (13) Georgia*

Nov 7   Vanderbilt*

Nov 14   at South Carolina*

Nov 21   Florida International

Nov 28   (21) Florida State

*SEC Opponents

Florida Hypothetic Schedule

Sept 5   Charleston Southern

Sept 12   Troy

Sept 19   Tennessee

Sept 26   at Central Florida*

Oct 10   at South Florida*

Oct 17   Arkansas

Oct 24   at Miami*

Oct 31   (13) Georgia

Nov 7   Florida Atlantic*

Nov 14   at South Carolina

Nov 21   Florida International*

Nov 28   (21) Florida State*

  *Realigned Conference Opponents

You will notice that in 2009, Florida had eight home games and only four road games. That is fairly typical of the big time programs that buy home games with teams like Troy, Charleston Southern and Florida International. You will also notice that

Florida's four road games are all required conference games.

In the "Hypothetic Schedule" you will notice that most of the same opponents have been retained. I simply placed Central Florida, South Florida, Miami and Florida Atlantic in spots occupied by Kentucky, LSU, Mississippi State and Vanderbilt. In a national championship playoff that requires teams to either place first or second in their conference to qualify, Florida could take some risks and play Texas or USC as an opener instead of Charleston Southern, a FCS (D-IA) program. The Gators would not be penalized if they lost an opener to USC.

Let's take a look at USC's 2009 schedule and compare it with a hypothetic schedule the Trojans could conceivably play in a new realigned conference:

USC 2009 Schedule

Sept 5   San Jose St.
Sept 12   at Ohio State
Sept 19   at Washington*
Sept 26   Washington St*
Oct 3   at California*
Oct 17   at Notre Dame
Oct 24   Oregon State*
Oct 31   at Oregon*
Nov 7   at Arizona State*
Nov 14   Stanford*
Nov 28   UCLA*
Dec 5   Arizona*
*Pac 10 Opponents

USC Hypothetic Schedule

Sept 5   San Jose St.*

Sept 12   at Ohio State

Sept 19   at Fresno State*

Sept 26   Washington St.

Oct 3   at California*

Oct 17   at Notre Dame

Oct 24   Hawaii*

Oct 31   at Oregon

Nov 7   at San Diego State*

Nov 14   Stanford*

Nov 28   UCLA*

Dec 5   Arizona

* Realigned Conference Opponents

You will notice that USC plays nine conference games in the Pac 10. Their three non-conference games for 2009 were San Jose State, Ohio State and Notre Dame. The hypothetic schedule was created by replacing Washington with Fresno State, Oregon State with Hawaii and replacing Arizona State with San Diego State. The hypothetic schedule still has the Trojans playing at Oregon and hosting Arizona. It looks as though USC fans would hardly see much difference in their home schedule. The most positive aspects of the hypothetic schedule is that USC would be visiting Fresno State and San Diego State which would greatly enhance those two programs.

Now let's take a look at Michigan's 2009 and hypothetic schedules:

Michigan 2009 Schedule

Sept 5   Western Michigan
Sept 12   Notre Dame
Sept 19   Eastern Michigan
Sept 26   Indiana*
Oct 3   at (24) Michigan State*
Oct 10   at (20) Iowa*
Oct 17   Delaware State
Oct 24   (8) Penn State*
Oct 31   at Illinois*
Nov 7   Purdue*
Nov 14   at Wisconsin*
Nov 21   (9) Ohio State*
* Big 10 Opponents

Michigan Hypothetic Schedule

Sept 5   Western Michigan*
Sept 12   Notre Dame
Sept 19   Eastern Michigan*
Sept 26   Indiana
Oct 3   at (24) Michigan State*
Oct 10   at (20) Iowa

Oct 17   Delaware State

Oct 24   (8) Penn State

Oct 31   at Central Michigan*

Nov 7   Minnesota*

Nov 14   at Wisconsin*

Nov 21   (9) Ohio State

* Realigned Conference Opponent

Many people I have talked to expressed the opinion that it wouldn't be football if Ohio State and Michigan did not play. Notice that this rivalry can survive conference realignment, as does the Michigan-Notre Dame rivalry. The major change is that Central Michigan is added and replaces Illinois in the hypothetic schedule.

We could go on and on with this exercise but I think the point has been made. The fans of the big powerhouse programs will not see that much difference in their home schedule. There will be plenty of great rivalry games for television. With fewer conference games, schools have more freedom to schedule more games in non-conference. Again a major difference in scheduling is the fact that schools like Central Michigan will get to host Michigan State and Michigan. This should boost ticket sales and may even encourage the enlargement of some stadiums.

CHAPTER EIGHT

PREDICTION: ATTENDANCE WOULD SKYROCKET

It takes a lot of courage to release the familiar and seemingly secure, to embrace the new. But there is no real security in what is no longer meaningful. There is more security in the adventurous and exciting, for in movement there is life, and in change there is power.

Alan Cohen

Those associated with the powerhouse Bowl Championship Series schools and conferences could argue that conference realignment would negatively impact the attendance of their home games. The evidence shows otherwise. A look at the NCAA's Single Game Team Report on Attendance for the 2008 season gives us information that would not support that argument.

The University of Michigan leads the nation in football game attendance year in and year out. Michigan stadium has the largest seating capacity of any stadium in the nation. A look at Michigan's single game attendance for the 2008 season shows that seven of the top twelve largest crowds in the country were at Michigan home games. The Michigan vs. Michigan State game drew the largest crowd in the nation with 110,146 in attendance. Not far behind was the crowd of 109,833 that attended the Wisconsin game.

With attendance figures like that, it is easy to see why some would say if it's not broke, don't fix it. If you will look a little closer at the list of the top crowds you will see that Michigan drew a crowd of 108,445 when they hosted non-BCS school Utah for a non-conference game. Michigan's non-conference clash with Toledo, also a non-BCS program, attracted 107,267 fans, the eleventh best attended game in the nation. My point is this; the attendance report shows that programs like Michigan, Penn State, Tennessee, Ohio State, Georgia, Texas, Alabama and the like are going to fill their stadium if they play a conference rival or a non-BCS school. So attendance will not be adversely affected if the conferences are realigned to include schools not previously in the traditional conferences.

A closer look at Southeastern Conference schools, Georgia, LSU and Alabama supports this premise. Georgia reported a crowd of 92,746 for their game with Central Michigan. That is the same number reported in attendance with SEC rival Alabama. LSU's home clash with SEC rival, Alabama drew a reported 93,039 fans, the Tigers' game with Troy University, a

Sun Belt Conference member, drew almost as many, 92,103.

Single Game Team Attendance Report[3]

Rank	Home Team	Opponent	Date	Attendance
1	Michigan	Michigan St.	25-OCT-08	110146
2	Penn St.	Michigan	18-OCT-08	110017
3	Penn St.	Michigan St.	22-NOV-08	109845
4	Michigan	Wisconsin	27-SEP-08	109833
5	Michigan	Illinois	04-OCT-08	109750
6	Penn St.	Illinois	27-SEP-08	109626
7	Penn St.	Indiana	15-NOV-08	108445
8	Michigan	Utah	30-AUG-08	108421
9	Penn St.	Oregon St.	06-SEP-08	108159
10	Michigan	Northwestern	15-NOV-08	107856
11	Michigan	Toledo	11-OCT-08	107267
12	Michigan	Miami (Ohio)	06-SEP-08	106724
13	Penn St.	Coastal Caro.	30-AUG-08	106577
14	Tennessee	Alabama	25-OCT-08	106138
14	Tennessee	Florida	20-SEP-08	106138
16	Ohio St.	Penn St.	25-OCT-08	105711
17	Ohio St.	Michigan	22-NOV-08	105564
18	Ohio St.	Purdue	11-OCT-08	105378
19	Ohio St.	Minnesota	27-SEP-08	105175
20	Penn St.	Temple	20-SEP-08	105106
21	Ohio St.	Youngstown St.	30-AUG-08	105011
22	Ohio St.	Ohio	06-SEP-08	105002
23	Ohio St.	Troy	20-SEP-08	102989
24	Tennessee	Kentucky	29-NOV-08	102388
25	Tennessee	Northern Ill.	04-OCT-08	99539
26	Tennessee	Wyoming	08-NOV-08	99489
27	Texas	Texas A&M	27-NOV-08	98621
28	Texas	Oklahoma St.	25-OCT-08	98518
29	Texas	Missouri	18-OCT-08	98383

---

5   *Single Game Team Report Attendance Bowl Subdivision.* Rep. NCAA, 5 Feb. 2009.
Web. 5 Feb. 2009.

30	Tennessee	Mississippi St.	18-OCT-08	98239
31	Tennessee	UAB	13-SEP-08	98205
32	Texas	Fla. Atlantic	30-AUG-08	98053
33	Texas	Arkansas	27-SEP-08	97833
34	Texas	Baylor	08-NOV-08	97715
35	Texas	Rice	20-SEP-08	97201
36	USC	Ohio St.	13-SEP-08	93607
37	USC	Penn St.	01-JAN-09	93293
38	LSU	Alabama	08-NOV-08	93039
39	LSU	Georgia	25-OCT-08	92904
40	Georgia	Georgia Tech	29-NOV-08	92746
40	Georgia	Central Mich.	06-SEP-08	92746
40	Georgia	Ga. Southern	30-AUG-08	92746
40	Georgia	Alabama	27-SEP-08	92746
40	Georgia	Tennessee	11-OCT-08	92746
40	Georgia	Vanderbilt	18-OCT-08	92746
46	LSU	Mississippi St.	27-SEP-08	92710
47	LSU	Mississippi	22-NOV-08	92649
48	Oklahoma	Texas	11-OCT-08	92182
49	Alabama	Arkansas St.	01-NOV-08	92138
49	Alabama	Mississippi St.	15-NOV-08	92138
49	Alabama	Tulane	06-SEP-08	92138
49	Alabama	Kentucky	04-OCT-08	92138
49	Alabama	Mississippi	18-OCT-08	92138
49	Alabama	Auburn	29-NOV-08	92138
49	Alabama	Western Ky.	13-SEP-08	92138

A look at Alabama's home crowds in 2008 shows that the Crimson Tide's non-conference games with Arkansas State, Tulane and Western Kentucky were as well attended as the games with SEC rivals Auburn, Mississippi and Mississippi State.

The conference realignment that the "True National Championship Playoff" calls for might be scary for some people, but the fear that it will adversely impact attendance for the powerhouse programs is unfounded. Even my alma mater, Sam Houston State (a FCS member a.k.a. IAA), drew 88,913 in 2006 when they visited Texas. The Buckeyes of Ohio State just drew 509 more fans in Austin!

The attendance records of the powerhouse programs show that fans will buy tickets to their favorite team's games, even if the opponent is not a conference rival or ranked team. So realigning the conferences to include new conference foes should not negatively impact ticket sales. In some cases, ticket sales may increase.

So what about those schools at the bottom of the attendance report? Let's consider a program that ranked in the last thirty for average attendance in 2008. Let's look at Rice University of Houston, Texas, a member of the Conference USA, a non-BCS or "second tier" conference. Rice's average attendance in 2008 was 20,179 which ranked 94th among schools in the Football Bowl Subdivision. Below are the attendance figures for Rice's six home games:

11/29/08	Houston*	35,534	W, 56-42
08/29/08	SMU*	23,164	W, 56-27
11/08/08	Army	19,243	W, 38-31
09/27/08	North Texas	16,885	W, 77-20
11/22/08	Marshall*	15,131	W, 35-10
10/18/08	Southern Miss.*	11,117	W, 45-40

* Conference USA game

It isn't any wonder why there were more fans for the Rice vs. Houston game than any other. Both universities are in Houston. It stands to reason that Southern Methodist of Dallas would draw more fans than Southern Mississippi. The sad reality is that the two teams that drew the smallest crowds are Rice's Conference USA members. Rice has to play them. I wouldn't think there is a huge herd of Marshall graduates in the Houston area. I am quite sure there are many Texas A&M exes living in the Houston area that would love to see their Aggies play in Rice Stadium, which seats 70,000.

On September 20, 2008, Rice played in front of 97,201 people when they played Texas in Austin. With the conference realignment that I am proposing, Rice would get to host Texas every other year. I have been to Rice Stadium when the Longhorns played Rice there. The place was packed with Longhorn fans, but the money for the tickets still goes to Rice athletics. The point is I think attendance for Rice home games would increase with conference realignment and attendance for Texas home games would remain at capacity.

Let's take a look at the University of Central Florida whose average attendance per game was 39,596 for 2008, which was 61st among the FBS schools. Central Florida plays in Conference USA and has a stadium that holds 45,301 spectators. UCF's home schedule with attendance is listed below:

09/06/08	South Florida	46,805	L, 31-24
10/04/08	SMU*	43,147	W, 31-17
08/30/08	So.Carolina St.	42,126	W, 17-0

11/08/08	Southern Miss.*	41,652	L, 17-6
11/02/08	East Carolina*	40,202	L, 13-10
11/29/08	UA-Birmingham*	23,644	L, 15-0

* Conference USA game

A brief look at the schedule and attendance report shows that UCF's best-attended game was a non-conference contest against South Florida. Undoubtedly, playing an in-state school created more interest and more spectators. South Carolina State, a Football Championship Series (IAA) program even outdrew UCF's conference opponents, Southern Mississippi, East Carolina and UAB. It seems that fans would rather see UCF play an in-state school even if that school is not a conference rival.

What affect would conference realignment have on UCF's attendance? I can't be sure, but I have to believe if UCF hosted Florida, Florida State, Miami and South Florida they would pack the stadium and be thinking about expanding their stadium or go back to playing some of their games in the 70,000 seat, Citrus Bowl.

In summary, regular season college football attendance should increase with conference realignment. The powerhouse programs would continue to produce sellouts no matter who is on their schedule. The schools such as Florida Atlantic, University of North Texas and Fresno State should see a huge increase in attendance when those schools host the traditional powerhouses in their home state.

Another factor that should increase fan interest and

attendance is that all 120 teams will actually have a chance to make the NCAA playoffs. Fans will maintain their interest even if their favorite team starts out with early non-conference losses. Conference games with in-state rivals will matter more when there is a national championship playoff berth at stake. With second place teams in each conference eligible for the playoffs, the outcomes of late season conference games should hold the attention of many fans.

Post-season Attendance Boost. Not only would conference realignment boost regular season attendance, the national championship playoff games will also draw more fans than the current post-season exhibition bowl games. Attendance at the exhibition bowl games has been an issue for most bowls. Much effort and money goes into promoting these exhibition games so that fans will be interested enough to attend games that don't mean anything.

Can you imagine the fan interest in playoff games that will lead to a national championship? These games would not have to be held in sunny California or Florida to attract fans. There would be enough interest in the game itself to sell tickets. All of the games would feature teams that have a legitimate chance of winning it all. The powerhouse programs like USC, Florida, Ohio State and Texas would possibly play multiple times rather than just one exhibition bowl game.

CHAPTER NINE
A 32 TEAM PLAYOFF AND WHY

Nothing ranks a man so quickly as his skill in selecting things that are really worthwhile. Every day brings the necessity of keen discrimination. Not always is it a choice between good and bad, but between good and best.

A.P. Gouthey

In the hypothetical playoff scenario that follows, I have chosen two teams from each of the realigned conferences and designated one as the conference winner and one as the runner-up. In the first round, conference winners play conference runners-up. Computer rankings and geezer coaches' polls are not necessary. It is also not necessary to subjectively seed any team in a bracket of eight, sixteen or thirty-two teams. Who would know if the two best teams were forced to play in the first round? Who knows which teams are the two best? You don't and neither do I.

Many people have discussed how well the NCAA basketball tournament is run and point to it as a model for football. Each year of the basketball tournament, there are some teams that feel like they were overlooked by the selection process. One year in the Division II national tournament I saw what I consider a harsh injustice occur. Tarleton State University defeated Abilene Christian both times they played in conference play and finished ahead of ACU in the league standings. The selection committee chose ACU over Tarleton even though both schools had at least twenty wins. At the time, the rationale given was that ACU had played a tougher schedule and had some wins in the early season against highly ranked teams. So in the opinion of someone, ACU was more deserving. As long as a subjective selection process is used, there will be players and fans that feel like they were treated unfairly and sometimes they will be right.

Hypothetical Playoff Scenario

First Round Games December 5, 2009 (Alternative date: December 12)

These games could be played at the conference winner's stadium provided it meets standards. Note: I have included the 2009 records of the teams involved. The teams that advance through each round do so based primarily on their 2009 BCS ranking.

Boise State (Winner 1) 12-0 vs. USC (Runner-up 2) 8-4

BYU (Winner 3) 10-2 vs. Nebraska (Runner-up 4) 9-3

Stanford (Winner 2) 8-4 vs. Oregon (Runner-up 1) 9-2

Iowa (Winner 4) 10-2 vs. Utah (Runner-up 3) 9-3

TCU (Winner 5) 12-0 vs. Houston (Runner-up 6) 10-2

LSU (Winner 7) 9-3 vs. Notre Dame (Runner-up 8) 6-6

Texas (Winner 6) 12-0 vs. Oklahoma State (Runner-up 5) 9-3

Northwestern (Winner 8) 8-4 vs. Missouri (Runner-up 7) 8-4

Central Michigan (Winner 9) 10-2 vs. Ohio State (Runner-up 10) 10-2

Penn State (Winner 11) 10-2 vs. Navy (Runner-up 12) 8-4

Cincinnati (Winner 10) 12-0 vs. Wisconsin (Runner-up 9) 9-3

West Virginia (Winner 12) 9-3 vs. Pittsburgh (Runner-up 11) 9-3

Virginia Tech (Winner 13) 9-3 vs. Clemson (Runner-up 14) 8-4

Alabama (Winner 15) 12-0 vs. Miami (Runner-up 16) 9-3

Georgia Tech (Winner 14) 10-2 vs. East Carolina (Runner-up 13) 8-4

Florida (Winner 16) 12-0 vs. Ole Miss (Runner-up 15) 8-4

Round of 16 Games December 19, 2009 (Alternative dates: December 12 or 26)

Boise State 13-0 vs. Nebraska 10-3

Oregon 11-2 vs. Iowa 11-2

TCU 13-0 vs. LSU 10-3

Texas 13-0 vs. Missouri 9-4

Ohio State 11-2 vs. Penn State 11-2

Cincinnati 13-0 vs. Pittsburgh 10-3

Clemson 9-4 vs. Alabama 13-0

Georgia Tech 11-2 vs. Florida 13-0

Quarterfinal Games January 1, 2010

Boise State 14-0 vs. Oregon 12-2

TCU 14-0 vs. Texas 14-0

Cincinnati 14-0 vs. Penn State 12-2

Alabama 14-0 vs. Florida 14-0

Semifinal Games January 9, 2010

Texas 15-0 vs. Boise State 15-0

Alabama 15-0 vs. Cincinnati 15-0

National Championship Game January 16, 2010

Alabama 16-0 vs. Texas 16-0

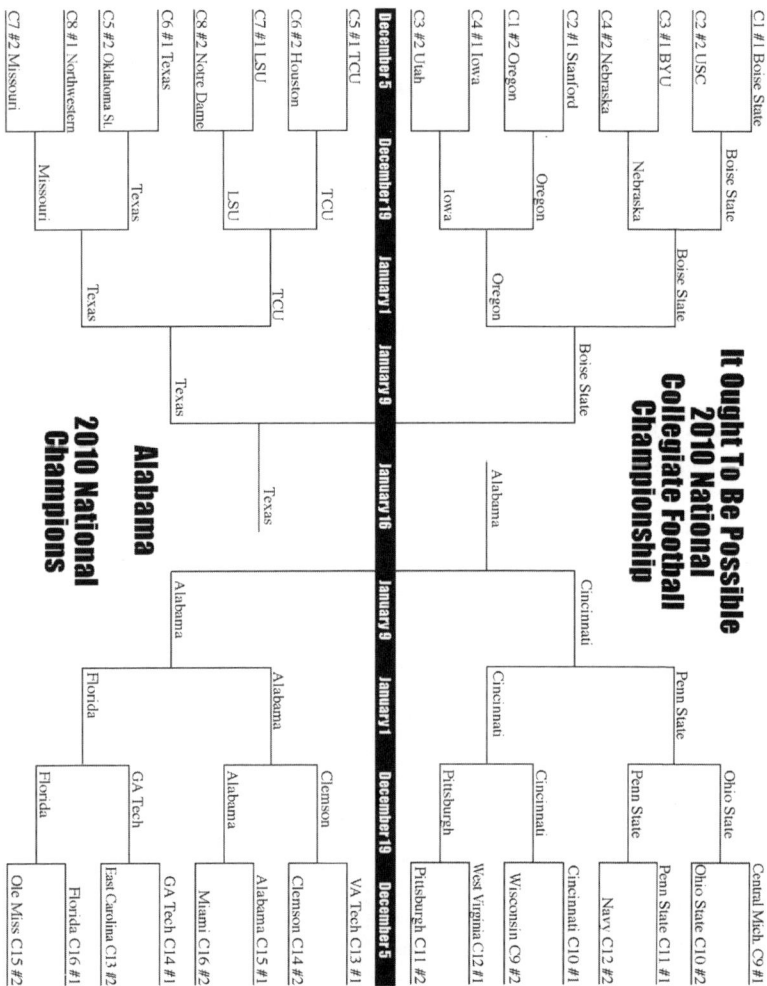

It Ought To Be Possible
2010 National
Collegiate Football
Championship

Alabama
2010 National
Champions

The dates of these games can be adjusted depending on priorities. My goal was to set up the quarterfinals on New Year's Day to pacify the traditionalist that wants to see great football on that day. All of the games in January should not interfere with classes since many schools will be between semesters. The December schedule could be adjusted according to priorities. If the priority is to wait for finals to be over to play the second round games, those games could be played December 26th. If you wanted to take a break for Christmas, then an adjustment could be made. The point is that this is doable. What makes it doable is that it really does not matter when you schedule these games there will be plenty of people willing to watch.

Most of the playoff scenarios that I have seen are usually four or eight team proposals. The problem with those proposals is that they will negatively impact the bowl games and not replace the money the current bowl games generate. A thirty-two team bracket requires playing thirty-one playoff games to complete. Those thirty-one games would surely generate more revenue than the current thirty-four exhibition bowl games. Two men who have worked within the system had this to say about money generated from a playoff:

"Financial reasons are a factor to a degree—probably more of a factor to some than to others. . . In and of itself, a playoff of some type would generate more money than the current BCS."

John Swofford
BCS Coordinator
ACC Commissioner
bcsfootball.org

"The current process is currently generating about 50 percent of what the value is."

Cedric Dempsey
NCAAPast President
December 17, 2002
CBSSPORTS.com

It is really hard to say how much more money a thirty-two team playoff would generate. I am satisfied that there would be a significant increase in gate receipts and television revenue. The real question about money is not how much, but for whom? The revenue made off of the NCAA basketball tournament is distributed to all schools based on how many sports they have and how many scholarships they give out.

So much of the revenue from the bowl games goes to the third parties that run the bowls. Dan Wetzel in his article for rivals.com entitled "The Bowl Boondoggle," reported that the Sugar Bowl spent $11.1 million to run the 2006 game. The Southeastern Conference operated its Championship Game for just $2.1 million in 2007. The point is money that could be going to schools is not.

If the NCAA would run the football playoffs, the schools could cash in even more by using their stadiums as playoff sites when practical. The largest football stadiums in the United States belong to universities. Pro stadiums do not come close to the seating capacity of the home fields of Penn State,

Michigan, Ohio State, Tennessee and Texas. After the first week of December, many of the college stadiums do not host football games, so therefore could be used to host playoff games. The state of South Carolina with two 80,000 seat stadiums could host playoff games between Virginia Tech and Alabama or Georgia Tech and Florida. The use of college stadiums could keep travel down and attendance up.

I have heard the excuse that a thirty-two team bracket would mean too many games for college athletes to play. That is a bogus excuse! High school players in Texas now play in a sixty-four team bracket at the end of their regular season. Many of these high school players are going both ways, on offense and defense, with less depth than the eighty plus rosters the college programs have. NFL rosters are made up of fifty-three players. So college rosters are bigger than both NFL rosters and the average high school roster. They should be able to play more games than the pros and high school teams. I am all for the safety of the athletes. I have never felt that playing a bowl game five or six weeks after your final regular season game was very safe anyway.

If you compare the total number of practice hours for thirty-two teams preparing for the playoffs with sixty-eight teams preparing for the thirty-four bowl games, it would seem there would be fewer practice hours with a playoff system. In the hypothetical playoff lineup, there would only be eight teams practicing after the third Saturday in December! That should reduce the number of injuries.

In this chapter we have presented a case for a thirty-two

team playoff and looked at a realistic yet hypothetical playoff scenario. In the process we have seen that the calendar would allow for five weekends of playoff football with negligible interference with the academic calendar. It is generally agreed upon by college officials that a playoff would generate more money if run by the NCAA.

CHAPTER TEN
ENOUGH EXCUSES ALREADY, ITS TIME

Any social organization must have members who respect authority in order to function and prosper and make life stable and better for everybody. Someone or some group must be in control, and others must be willing to accept their decisions.

Jay Mikes
Coach and Author

Those who serve the BCS kool-aid or benefit from the current system would like you to believe that a playoff would undermine the regular season. Let's look at this reasoning. BCS advocates say that college football has the best regular season in all of football because in order to be a national champion, a team must have a perfect (undefeated) or near perfect (maybe one loss) season. With the current ranking system of polls it has played out that way. Is that really good?

1. One result of this "goal of a perfect season" is that many teams set schedules to avoid getting upset. If one loss

can ruin your national championship goal, it does not make sense to schedule tough games on the road or at home. So schools have learned to work the system. Did you see Florida's 2009 schedule of eight home games and four road games? Did you see that Florida opened up with Charleston Southern of the Football Championship Subdivision? Does scheduling teams that have very little chance of winning in your stadium make for an exciting regular season or do exciting games make a regular season exciting?

2. If a team must go undefeated through the regular season in order to have a chance to play for a national championship, half of the teams are out of the running after the first weekend. When teams can lose games and still play for their conference championship and/or a berth in a playoff, more teams will be in the hunt and there will be more meaningful games in each conference.

3. College, and hopefully college athletics, is supposed to be about learning. There would be more learning involved in a season in which one loss does not doom your team. A team can learn more from losses against tough opponents than it can from lopsided wins. When I coached, I wanted players to learn from playing as tough a non-conference schedule as possible. I believed this would help us reach the goal of a conference championship which qualified us for the playoffs. If my team had to go undefeated to make the championship game, I would have scheduled easier opponents in non-conference and then hoped we could take care

of our conference foes. More learning will take place in a competitive season, when more teams have more opportunities to reach their goal of a postseason playoff and ultimately a true national championship.

The excuse that college football's regular season would be undermined with the establishment of playoffs is unfounded. Playoffs are going to be far more exciting with more teams being involved. Are we going to believe BCS conference commissioners, who have much to lose with a playoff system, or are we going use our own sense of reasoning?

Another excuse given for maintaining the current system is the wonderful 100 years of the bowl system. Wonderful for whom and wonderful compared to what? The system has been wonderful for the Pac 10, Big 10, SEC, Notre Dame and more recently the Big XII. The exhibition bowl system has been good for bowl directors and the hospitality businesses located in the cities of Pasadena, Miami, New Orleans, Dallas and Phoenix. A playoff conducted by the NCAA should bring in more money directly to the schools because it should be run more efficiently than the third-party-run bowl system.

Are exhibition bowl games really that wonderful for the players? Sure, there is the travel to a warm climate, hospitality of the locals for the players, amenities etc. What about the game itself? First of all, except for the BCS championship game, there is really nothing riding on these games, except reputation. In many instances, the incentive to win for one of the teams is greater than for the other team participating. Two examples are

Boise State's now famous Fiesta Bowl victory over Oklahoma
and Utah's Sugar Bowl victory over Alabama.

With all due respect for the Boise State players, coaches
and their entire program, the Broncos had everything to gain
and nothing to lose when they played Oklahoma on January
1, 2007. The Boise State players had more to be excited about
than the Sooner players. The Broncos were undefeated, playing
for respect from the media and pollsters. The Sooners, on the
other hand, were most likely disappointed they were not playing
in the BCS championship game. Players that sign to play with
Oklahoma expect to play for the BCS championship in January.
Boise State players were, no doubt, ecstatic to have a shot to
play Oklahoma. The result is Oklahoma's coaches were faced
with the challenge of inspiring their team to perform at its best
against a team that had a psychological edge because the game
was an exhibition. In a playoff game, both teams would have
been playing for the same thing; the next round of the playoffs
and eventually a true national championship.

In 2008, Alabama was ranked number one for the last
month of the regular season. The Crimson Tide players dreamt
of playing for the BCS title throughout the season. Losing
to Florida the first weekend of December ruined Alabama's
dreams. Instead of playing in the BCS championship game, the
Crimson Tide was assigned to play Utah in the Sugar Bowl.
Alabama was most likely disappointed to be in the Sugar Bowl.
Utah was undefeated and felt it deserved to play Florida for the
BCS title. The Utes were angry and anger can motivate! Again,
the incentives for the teams were different. Alabama was placed

in the difficult position of trying to get up for a game against a team that had more to prove. A playoff can remedy this situation.

Over the one-hundred-year history of the exhibition bowl games, many people have developed some warm fuzzy feelings about their experiences. The cities and the people that have hosted these events have prospered financially. Reported salaries of the directors of a bowl game are in excess of $400,000. These same cities or other cities could still prosper from the crowds that are attracted to the playoff games.

The great city of Atlanta hosts the Chick-fil-A Bowl each year. This bowl was once called the Peach Bowl, but today it's easier to find a Chick-fil-A restaurant in Atlanta than it is Georgia peaches! The organizers of the Chick-fil-A Bowl have started a new tradition. It is the Chick-Fil-A Kickoff Classic that started Labor Day weekend in 2008. Alabama and Clemson played in the inaugural game, which was a great success. I think it is a great idea and could be the answer for our bowl cities trying to adjust to the public demands for a playoff.

Imagine, if you will, instead of cities and bowl committees trying to host exhibition games at the end of the season in December and January, they could host the very first game of the season, Labor Day weekend. Fans could come by the thousands to support their team as they kickoff the season with great momentum and enthusiasm. Every fan's team would be undefeated at this point! This would be a great time to travel, the last getaway before everyone gets too settled in at school. It could mean one last trip to the beach or even the mountains at the end of the summer. What would be better about the exhibition bowl games being played the first weekend in September is that the northern cities could also get in on the action. Cities like Chicago, Philadelphia, Denver and Boston have been left out of the bowl action but could cash in by staging games for fans that would be interested in traveling to the cooler north.

Football fans are calling for a playoff and will grow tired of a bowl system that hinders a true national championship. A national championship playoff can and will create more excitement for the game of college football. A national championship playoff will be better for the players, the coaches and the fans.

CHAPTER ELEVEN
SO LETS TALK ABOUT MONEY

Progress always involves risk; you can't steal second base and keep your foot on first.

Frederick Wilcox

Time and time again in the last two years, I have been told that the big issue surrounding a college football playoff is the money. I heard, "Things will never change, because there is too much money being made in the current bowl system." It seems to be all about money. People would say, "Your plan sounds fair, but if it doesn't make more money, it won't matter."

Since my background is coaching and playing sports, my first goal was to develop a plan that allowed for players and coaches to play for a championship on the field. To be truthful, how much money the playoff made was secondary to creating a more equitable plan. I was not concerned with what the media and fans would think. I felt if you design a system that helps the game and the players, the fans and media would still be loyal. I believed if you did the right thing, then the money issue would take care of itself.

The longer I studied the issues, the more convinced I became that the new system would generate more revenue for colleges across the nation. I found that I was not the only one that felt this way. Homer Rice of Georgia Tech speaking at the 1988 NCAA Convention, while discussing the need for a Division I-A football playoff said:

> It seems like an impossibility to contain costs. Therefore, we have to look for more income. If you go back through history, there's always been a bonanza. Something happens. We started foundations to raise money for scholarships. Then, we added student fees for nonrevenue sports. Television for football increased, then television for basketball jumped fantastically. Money from NCAA championships increased. Each time, it seemed there was something for us. Now, I don't see anything except the football playoff system so we can make the next jump. In essence, that's what it's all about.

What I respect about Homer Rice's comments is that he seems to be concerned about college athletics as a whole, not just his school. Homer Rice was a fine coach before he became an athletic director. Apparently, Mr. Rice believed that a playoff would greatly increase revenue and that revenue would benefit many.

Distinguished attorney Barry Brett, speaking before the

Senate Judiciary Committee, on July 9, 2009, stated, "It is estimated that a playoff system would produce more than twice the revenue of the BCS system." In his written statement to Senator Orin Hatch, Brett said estimates for a playoff would be in excess of $375 million. Brett is just one of many that believe a playoff will produce more revenue than the bowl system.

Darren Rovell of *CNBC's Sport Business Reporter*,[4] estimated that television money for a six-game playoff would be worth $160 million and would more than double, with a network paying $640 million for a four-year playoff package. Rovell's estimate used the existing bowl structure. He estimated quarterfinal games would be worth $22 million each, semifinal games would be worth $28 million and the final would be worth $38 million. If a six game playoff would bring in $160 million, imagine what a thirty-one game playoff would generate.

I have to estimate a thirty-one game playoff would be worth between $300 and 400 million. Here is how I calculated my estimate. The closest thing we have seen to a first round of a playoff would be the super-conference championship games. So let's explore the history and economics of these conference championship games.

Those conferences desiring to attract lucrative television contracts expanded the size of their conferences and then split into two divisions. A split-division conference requires the two divisional champions to play a conference championship game, similar to the first round of a thirty-two team playoff. Historically,

---

4   Darren Rovell, *College Football Playoffs: I'll Say They're Worth $160 Million a Year*, CNBC, January 9, 2008, http://www.cnbc.com/id/22570730).

these games have been very profitable for the Southeastern Conference. In fact in 2008, the SEC made $14 million off of their conference championship game held in Atlanta. The SEC championship match up of # 1 Alabama against Florida was the highest rated TV game of 2008. The Big XII, Conference USA, Mid-American and the Sun Belt conferences also use a championship game.

Let's be *very* conservative and say that first round games would make $7 million, that's half of the income from the SEC championship game. Multiply sixteen times seven million and you get $112 million for the first round games. The eight second round games should make more than first round games, so let's say $10 million each for second round games, which totals $80 million. The four quarterfinal games that could be scheduled on New Year's Day would conservatively bring in $15 million each for a total of $60 million. Let's say $20 million for the semifinals and a very conservative $30 million for the championship game.

16 First round games @ $7 million each   = $112,000,000.00
8 Second round games @ $10 million each = $80,000,000.00
4 Quarterfinal games @ $15 million each   = $60,000,000.00
2 Semifinal games @ $20 million each   = $40,000,000.00
Championship Game @ 30 million   = $30,000,000.00
                                  Total $322,000,000.00

Rovell's estimate of television revenue for the last three rounds is much higher than mine. If we inject Rovell's estimates, we can add an additional $52 million to my estimate, for a grand total of $374 million. These estimates support the notion that a playoff would just about double the revenue that the bowls are generating. The point is that a playoff should generate more money for the colleges in the Football Bowl Subdivision than the bowl system.

Former NCAA Executive Director, Cedric Dempsey was quoted by Scott M. Reid, in the *Orange County Register* as saying, "The current bowl system needs overhauling, but the people that control college football don't want to give up that control, control of all that money." The people that Dempsey is talking about are the "third party" bowl associations/directors, conference commissioners, corporate and television sponsors. Collectively, they get to slice the pie. They serve up different size pieces based on conference affiliation. It is generally assumed that if a playoff is implemented, the NCAA would run it. Since the NCAA is made up of member schools, the organization would answer and be accountable to those schools.

In reviewing the literature about the issue of a college playoff, I found that two different writers had described the college football bowl system as a "boondoggle." One writer was Dan Wetzel in the aforementioned, *The Bowl Boondoggle.* Just what is a boondoggle? The *Encarta World English Dictionary* defines boondoggle as *"a **wasteful pursuit:** an activity or project that is unnecessary and wasteful of time or money, especially one undertaken for personal or political gain."*

In *The Bowl Boondoggle,* Dan Wetzel bluntly revealed how much waste there is when third parties run post-season college football. Consider the following information Wetzel gathered on the workings of the Sugar Bowl:

Scanning recent tax documents, the Sugar Bowl spent:

- $1.3 million in employee salaries in 2006, including $453,399 in total compensation for CEO Paul Hoolahan
- $494,177 in unspecified "entertainment" (in 2005)
- $455,781 on unspecified "appropriations" (in 2006)
- $348,487 in "Sugar Bowl entertainment" (in 2006)
- $188,305 on "Hall of Fame" (in 2005)
- $176,277 on "media relations" (in 2006)
- $118,004 on "decorations" (in 2006)
- $114,666 on "committee meetings" (in 2006)
- $84,255 on "conference relations" (in 2006)
- $82,884 on "other expenses" (in 2006)
- $60,932 on "gifts and bonuses" (in 2005)
- $58,995 on "liaison" (in 2006)
- $46,017 on "conference meetings" (in 2006)

Overall the Sugar Bowl spent $11.1 million in 2006 alone. The SEC operated its 2007 Championship Game (in effect a bowl game) for just $2.1 million. The ACC managed to pull off its 2006 title game for $1.2 million. . . . It's not easy making a *single, three-and-a-half hour football game* cost over $11 million . . . It's not just the Sugar Bowl. The Orange Bowl did over $17.9 million in revenue and the Rose Bowl over $10 million according to 2007 tax records. Both spent almost all of it[5]

Writer Scott M. Reid of the Orange County Register had this to say in 2007:

. . . the main obstacle standing in the way of a playoff is the bowl system itself, a billion-dollar-a-year industry operated primarily by tax exempt bowl committees who have spent decades and millions of dollars nurturing relationships with influential friends on university campuses, conference headquarters, state houses and the halls of power in Washington, D.C. . . . Corporate sponsors, conference commissioners, administrators, coaches with bowl bonuses in their contracts and boosters and university

---

5   Dan Wetzel, *The Bowl Boondoggle,* Yahoo Sports, December 18, 2008, http://rivals.yahoo.com/ncaa/football/news?slug=dw-bowls121808

trustees are accustomed to holiday rounds of golf in Arizona or Florida. Plus, local economies in bowl cities all have stakes in a bowl system that would be threatened by a playoff tournament.

Reid also reported:

- That in 2007, twenty-two bowls were operated by organizations that benefit from tax-exempt status

- Those twenty-two bowls generated $800 million in gross receipts from 2001 to 2007

- Compensation to officers at bowl committees with non-profit status has more than doubled since 2001

- According to documents filed with the U.S. Senate and House of Representatives, a fund created by the four BCS games has sent more than $500,000 to a lobbying firm run by J.C. Watts, a former Oklahoma Congressman and Sooners quarterback.[6]

What I gleaned from this information is that while the big, powerful, third party bowl associations manage to provide

---

6   Scott M. Reid, *Special Report: College football's money bowl,*" *Orange County Register*, December 25, 2007.

big payouts for the preferred conferences, there is a lot of waste. The NCAA and all its member schools have proven they can run and stage their own football games. The third parties are not necessary. If member schools would allow the NCAA to direct a championship, the revenue generated would not have to go through third party hands and more money could find its way back to the student-athletes and their institutions.

So how would the NCAA use the money generated from a college football championship? The NCAA website, www.ncaa.org reads, "Approximately 95 percent of the revenue that the NCAA receives from television/marketing rights fees and championships is returned to the membership in the form of direct payments and event services." In the *2008-09 Revenue Distribution Plan* posted on the NCAA website, I learned that funds are distributed through the following programs:

1. "Academic Enhancement—approximately $20,667,000 is allocated for enhancement of academic-support programs for student-athletes at Division I institutions. Reported uses of the fund, were tutoring ($4,626,891), personnel ($10,798,672), computer services, academic programs and equipment.

2. Basketball Fund—in 2008-09, a total $154.7 million was distributed to all schools playing Division I basketball.

3. Conference Grants—a total of $7,467,000 is allocated for grants to Division I men's and women's basketball-playing conferences.

These grant funds must be used to maintain, enhance or implement programs and services in each of the following areas:

a) Men's and women's officiating programs: permissible uses include the improvement of officiating programs in all sports, as opposed to just in men's and women's basketball.

b) Enhancement of conference compliance and enforcement programs.

c) Heightening the awareness of athletics staffs and student-athletes to programs associated with drug use, and assisting coaches, athletics administrators and student-athletes in this regard.

d) Enhancement of opportunities: employment, professional development, career advancement and leadership/ management training in intercollegiate athletics for ethnic minorities.

e) Development of conference gambling education programs.

4. Grant-in-aid—broad-based distribution is made to all Division I institutions on the basis of the number of varsity sports sponsored (weighted one-third, totaling $51.6 million) and the number of athletics grants-in-aid awarded (weighted two-thirds, totaling $103.1 million).

5. Special Assistance—a total of $13,383,000 is sent to conference offices in early August to assist student-athletes in Division I with special financial needs. The guiding principles of the fund are to meet the student-athletes' needs of an emergency or essential nature for which financial assistance otherwise is not available.

6. Sports Sponsorship—in the 2007-08 distribution, for sports sponsored beginning with the 14th, an institution received approximately $26,123 per sport (i.e., an institution sponsoring 16 total sports received $78,369; an institution sponsoring 24 sports received $287,353).

7. Student-athlete Opportunity—the Student-Athlete Opportunity Fund is intended to provide direct benefits to student-athletes or their families as determined by conference offices. As a guiding principle, the fund shall be used to assist student-athletes in meeting financial needs that arise in conjunction with participation in intercollegiate athletics, enrollment in an academic curriculum or that recognize academic achievement."

In addition, the NCAA funds championships in eighty-eight sports. Travel expenses for the participants of those championships are paid by the NCAA. So a tennis player from

New Mexico State that qualifies for the national finals in Georgia will be assured of being able to participate.

The NCAA is a fine organization of member schools. The organization has proven it can conduct a profitable basketball playoff and distribute money back to the member schools and its student-athletes. In contrast, the bowl system has shown it cares little about fairness and is more interested in making money *off* of college sports than *for* college sports.

Some NCAA member schools are thriving in the current atmosphere. They were in the right place at the right time when conferences were formed. These schools benefit from being in densely populated areas where they can draw great crowds and TV viewership. Other NCAA member schools are struggling to maintain sponsorship of non-revenue sports. There is definitely a two-tier system, the haves and the have-nots. The bowl system, with its payouts to the preferred conferences and schools, widens the gap.

It seems obvious to me that a national football playoff will bring in more revenue to members schools if the NCAA would run the playoff system. Currently the organization lacks synergy because some schools or groups of schools are unwilling to submit to the authority of the NCAA. If the automatic-qualifying BCS schools and their conference representatives choose to use the power and popularity gained from the bowl system and television networks, to maintain their advantage, change will be extremely difficult.

"The BCS is and always will be about the business of preserving a monopoly of the power football conferences, which have little if any interest in sharing the wealth with everyone else. A true playoff system would certainly provide an opportunity for an enormous payoff for everyone, just like the NCAA basketball playoffs. But that would mean sharing all that cash on a more equitable basis with the entire upper tier of Division I football schools."

Bryan Burwell
St. Louis Post-Dispatch

12/08/2009

". . . the top hundred football programs have their own thing and then there's I-AA. It's a completely different animal. And they don't have a system that would allow a smaller school to get into their spotlight in the BCS. They know what they're doing as far as (a) monopoly. That's why I think our tournament has captured America, is because everybody can get in it. Everybody can identify. Everyone's got a chance."

Coach Mike Krzyzewski
Eve of NCAA Basketball Championship
Matchup with Butler University

CHAPTER TWELVE
IT OUGHT TO BE POSSIBLE

It's not hard to make decisions when you know what your values are.

Roy Disney, American Film Writer,
Nephew of Walt Disney

I have attempted to refute all the possible reasons for maintaining the current football competition and conference structure. The opinion polls show that most football fans want to see the bowl system changed. Understandably, change will not come without resistance from those parties that thrive in the current system.

A fair and just system was my goal. Hopefully, I have shown that more schools and more student-athletes will benefit from realignment of the conferences and a thirty-two team playoff. I know that some of those conferences are institutions, in place for a long time and steeped in tradition. Some people would prefer to maintain the status quo and not think about the programs and the players that must overcome the obstacles created by the current system.

Albert Einstein said, *"In matters of truth and justice, there is no difference between large and small problems, for issues concerning the treatment of people are all the same."* President Obama and several members of Congress have been criticized in the media for making college football a political issue, when government seemed to have bigger problems. Rep. Joe Barton of Texas said, *"We are trying to create enough public pressure to cause them to switch voluntarily to a playoff system."*

Since Congress allows the big-time college athletic programs to receive tax-deductible donations as tax-exempt, non-profits, Congress has a responsibility to have the Justice Department investigate when citizens question the practices of non-profit corporations. The Justice Department should look at the business practices of the colleges and compare it to what is reasonable. Any informed, fair-minded individual can see that there are some unfair practices at work in college athletics, when compared with the standards of fairness established by state high school associations and America's professional leagues. As Einstein suggests, if it involves justice and the treatment of people, it warrants the attention of our nation's leaders.

In the months after developing my ideas, I could not help but ask the question, "Would the athletic directors and coaches of the automatic-qualifying BCS conferences want to be treated the way their counterparts of the non-automatic qualifying BCS conferences are being treated?" I believe the answer is a resounding "no." I googled "The Golden Rule" and found the following statements by Dr. Harry J. Gensler of John Carroll University:

> The golden rule is best interpreted as saying: "Treat others only in ways that you're willing to be treated in the same exact situation." To apply it, you'd imagine yourself in the exact place of the other person on the receiving end of the action. If you act in a given way toward another, and yet are unwilling to be treated that way in the same circumstances, then you violate the rule.
>
> To apply the golden rule adequately, we need knowledge and imagination. We need to *know* what effect our actions have on the lives of others. And we need to be able to *imagine* ourselves, vividly and accurately, in the other person's place on the receiving end of the action. With knowledge, imagination, and the golden rule, we can progress far in our moral thinking. . . . If we violate the golden rule, then we're violating the spirit of fairness and concern that lie at the heart of morality.

Dr. Gensler points out that President John F. Kennedy used the Golden Rule when he appealed to U.S. citizens in an anti-segregation speech in 1963. Kennedy stated that the heart of the matter was "whether we are going to treat our fellow Americans as we want to be treated." It is a good question to ask ourselves each and every day. Some people will scoff at the notion of applying the Golden Rule to competitive sports, but as Kennedy said in his 1963 speech, "This is one country. It has become one country because all of us and all the people who came here had an equal chance to develop their talents."

President Kennedy repeated the statement, "It ought to be possible" several times throughout the speech. The phrase was very effective in making the point that things are not as they should be, but could be if people would choose to treat others the way they would want to be treated. Applying the Golden Rule to the issue of college athletics could bring about the changes so many people involved in sports long for.

If state high school athletic associations can conduct championship football playoffs, it ought to be possible for a collegiate athletic association to do the same. If every major professional sports league in this country can conduct playoffs, without computer rankings and subjective polls, it ought to be possible for college presidents to find a way to do the same. If a group of professional football team investors can agree to share revenue for the good of all the franchises in the NFL, it ought to be possible for a group of college presidents, who have no monetary investment, to agree to do the same.

In 1970, the National Football League merged with the American Football League. I remember my father saying that more teams meant more jobs for more players. Dad believed it was good for football. The merger involved the realignment of conferences or divisions. To complete the merger, the Pittsburgh Steelers, Baltimore Colts and Cleveland Browns of the "old guard" NFL agreed to play in the newly formed conference with the ten AFL franchises, such as the New York Jets, Buffalo Bills and Oakland Raiders. If these franchises could agree to make changes to conference alignments, for the good of professional football, it ought to be possible for college presidents to empower the NCAA to align conferences to benefit the most schools and put an end to the exclusionary practices involving conference membership. It ought to be possible for a college program, new to the Football Bowl Subdivision, to be aligned in a conference with schools that have rich traditions and have all the rights and responsibilities of the established programs.

When the Rose Bowl started in 1902, many people still made their living in the horse and buggy industry. Then a better idea, known as the automobile, came along. If people can adjust to the changes created by the invention of the automobile, it ought to be possible for the bowl associations to adjust to the world of college football playoffs.

Richard Barrett is an internationally known culture consultant and keynote speaker on values and cultural transformation. Barrett explains, "When organizations unite around a shared set of values, they become more flexible, less hierarchical, less bureaucratic, and they develop an enhanced capacity for collective action." It really comes down to the ability of American institutions of higher learning to unite behind a shared set of values. When college presidents can agree to base their decision-making around the values of equal opportunity and fairness, I am confident that students, student-athletes, coaches and fans across the great land will be the beneficiaries.

And what does the Lord require of you?
To act justly and to love mercy
And to walk humbly with your God.
Micah 6:8 (NIV)

This is what the Lord says:
"Let not the wise man boast of his wisdom
or the strong man boast of his strength
or the rich man boast of his riches,
but let him who boasts boast about this:
that he understands and knows me,
that I am the Lord, who exercises kindness,
justice and righteousness on earth,
for in these I delight,"
declares the Lord.
Jeremiah 9:23-24 (NIV)

ACKNOWLEDGEMENTS

The genesis of this book has to be my introduction to football by my father. His love for competition and the lessons that could be learned from it was contagious. Whether it was in the living room, in front of the television, or telling stories about great players on the way to watch high school football, my father taught me the value of fair competition.

My mother also taught me some valuable lessons about fairness. The last portions of homemade ice cream, cake or lemon pie can be sources of conflict in a family of five scrappy boys. Mom used these teachable moments so well. When two brothers had designs on the last portion of pie, Mom would instruct one to slice the pie into two pieces. After the pie was divided, Mom allowed the other brother to choose which slice he wanted. We all learned how to slice pie into two equal portions. It was a fair way to deal with two boys who thought they had a right to something someone else made.

Although I have yet to meet Michael Josephson, his book,

Pursuing Victory with Honor: the Ultimate Sportsmanship Tool Kit, played a huge role in this book by stressing how sport impacts the values of society. Another source of inspiration was the Positive Coaching Alliance (positivecoach.org) that seeks to "transform youth sports, so sports can transform youth."

I would also like to acknowledge and thank two distinguished scholars who were considerate enough to take time to advise an old coach. I sought out Dr. Jay Coakley and Dr. Andrew Zimbalist at the *Scholarly Colloquium on College Sports* at the 2010 NCAA Convention and both went out of their way to listen to my ideas. Dr. Zimbalist was kind enough to share his paper, *The BCS, Anti-Trust and Public Policy* before it had been published.

Thanks goes out to my friend, Bobby McVey of BMc Graphics for designing the quality maps and the bracket that helps readers visualize the possibility for a playoff.

Heartfelt thanks to Cecil Eager, a former college athletic director, who encouraged me to persist in the face of discouragement. Throughout the writing, it was Cecil's confidence in my ideas that kept nudging me. Thanks to Tad Danner who saw the value in my plan and suggested I put in a book.

Finally, thanks to my wife, Marie, for enduring the endless discussion about a topic so far off her radar. She deserves better.

APPENDIX A: THE BACKUP PLAN

POOL PLAY FOR A CHAMPIONSHIP PLAYOFF

If indeed conference realignment is impossible because schools refuse to submit to the authority of the NCAA, there is an alternative. It is pool play which allows for every school to earn its way into a playoff bracket, with minimal use of polls or rankings. If schools insist on remaining aligned in the current conferences, the NCAA could conduct a national football championship using pool play during the regular season to determine the participants of a thirty-two team playoff. The nuts and bolts of the plan:

1. All 120 FBS schools would be divided into thirty groups or pools of four schools. The pools would be formed as objectively as possible, using geographic location to determine groupings. When possible, schools in the same state would be grouped together.

2. Each school would be instructed to schedule games with the teams assigned to its pool. The NCAA would

determine the location of the games. All schools would be subject to playing some games on the road during pool play. That means USC may be required to play at San Diego State or Hawaii. Schools would still play in the current conferences and play for a conference championship.

3. The winners of each of the thirty pools would be placed in a thirty-two team bracket. The two remaining spots in the bracket would be filled by two at-large teams selected by a selection committee. This is not ideal, but the numbers just don't work at this time. If FBS had 128 schools, thirty-two pools could be created and there would be no need for a selection committee.

4. The hypothetical pools that follow were created objectively, using geographic proximity. Every effort was made to have in-state schools play each other. This is especially important to those schools relatively new to the FBS or those schools that have been in the non-automatic qualifying conferences in order to have a chance to host other in-state schools. In pool play, Alabama will not be able to avoid having to play at Troy or UA-Birmingham. Schools such as East Carolina, Central Florida, North Texas and Fresno State should be able to get a financial boost when it hosts the flagship schools in its respective state.

5. The first round matchups and subsequent results are hypothetical using the 2009 results and rankings to determine "winners."

The Thirty Championship Pools

1. Washington, Washington State, Idaho, Boise State
2. Oregon, Oregon State, Nevada, Nevada-Las Vegas
3. Southern California, UCLA, San Diego State, Hawaii
4. Stanford, California, Fresno State, San Jose State,
5. Utah, Brigham Young, Utah State, Air Force
6. Arizona, Arizona State, New Mexico, New Mexico State
7. Colorado, Colorado State, Nebraska, Wyoming
8. Iowa, Iowa State, Kansas, Kansas State
9. Illinois, Northern Illinois, Kentucky, Western Kentucky
10. Oklahoma, Oklahoma State, Tulsa, Missouri
11. Arkansas State, Arkansas, TCU, Baylor
12. Texas A&M, Houston, Rice, Texas Tech,
13. Louisiana State, Tulane, LA Tech, LA-Lafayette
14. SMU, North Texas, Texas, Texas-El Paso
15. Notre Dame, Purdue, Indiana, Ball State
16. Michigan, Western Michigan, Wisconsin, Minnesota
17. Michigan State, Eastern Michigan, Central Michigan, Northwestern
18. Ohio State, Ohio, Toledo, Akron,
19. Cincinnati, Bowling Green, Miami of OH, Kent State
20. Louisville, West Virginia, Marshall, Navy
21. Syracuse, Buffalo, Army, Boston College
22. Connecticut, Penn State, Pitt, Temple
23. Virginia, Virginia Tech, Maryland, Rutgers
24. Tennessee, Memphis, Middle Tennessee, Vanderbilt

25. Clemson, Georgia, Georgia Tech, Duke
26. North Carolina, NC State, East Carolina, Wake Forest
27. Troy, Auburn, Alabama, Alabama-Birmingham,
28. Ole Miss, Miss. State, So. Miss, Louisiana-Monroe
29. Florida State, Florida, Central Florida, South Carolina
30. Miami, South Florida, Florida International, Florida Atlantic

Hypothetical Pool Winners with First Round Matchups

Boise State (Pool 1 Winner) vs. Oregon (Pool 2 Winner)

USC (Pool 3 Winner) vs. California (Pool 4 Winner)

BYU (Pool 5 Winner) vs. Arizona (Pool 6 Winner)

Iowa (Pool 7 Winner) vs. Nebraska (Poole 8 Winner)

Kentucky (Pool 9 Winner) vs. Oklahoma (Pool 10 Winner)

TCU (Pool 11 Winner) vs. Houston (Pool 12 Winner)

LSU (Pool 13 Winner) vs. Texas (Pool 14 Winner)

Notre Dame (Pool 15 Winner) vs. Pittsburgh
(At-large selection # 1)

Wisconsin (Pool 16 Winner) vs. Central Michigan
(Pool 17 Winner)

Ohio State (Pool 18 Winner vs. Cincinnati (Pool 19 Winner)

West Virginia (Pool 20 Winner) vs. Boston College
(Pool 21 Winner)

Penn State (Pool 22 Winner) vs. Virginia Tech (Pool 23 Winner)

Tennessee (Pool 24 Winner) vs. Georgia Tech (Pool 25 Winner)

East Carolina (Pool 26 Winner) vs. Alabama (Pool 27 Winner)
Ole Miss (Pool 28 Winner) vs. Florida (Pool 29 Winner)
Miami (Pool 30 Winner) vs. Clemson (At-large selection #2)

Second Round Matchups (Hypothetical)

Boise State vs. USC
BYU vs. Iowa
Oklahoma vs. TCU
Texas vs. Pittsburgh
Wisconsin vs. Cincinnati
West Virginia vs. Penn State
Georgia Tech vs. Alabama
Miami vs. Florida

Quarterfinals

Boise State vs. Iowa
TCU vs. Texas
Cincinnati vs. Penn State
Alabama vs. Florida

Semifinals

Boise State vs. Texas
Cincinnati vs. Alabama

National Championship Game

Texas vs. Alabama

Pool play offers an alternative to the conference realignment I have proposed. The current conference structure with its history of exclusivity could be maintained. Schools could continue to play their conference schedule and vie for a conference championship. However, performance in pool play would earn a school the right to play in the postseason national championship.

This is a backup plan. It is an alternative that is easier to implement and causes less disruption to the current system. Today's conferences with their illogically and politically conceived memberships could coexist with pool play. Membership in one of the automatic-qualifying conferences would no longer be as important. A prospective student-athlete would not have to choose a school in one of the preferred conferences to ensure he has a chance to play for a national title.

APPENDIX 2:
SUPER BOWL VS. BCS CHAMPIONSHIP GAME

NFL TEAMS PARTICIPATING IN THE SUPER BOWL DURING THE BCS ERA

Date	Champion	Score	Runner-up
January 31, 1999	Denver Broncos	34–19	Atlanta Falcons
January 30, 2000	St. Louis Rams	23–16	Tennessee Titans
January 28, 2001	Baltimore Ravens	34–7	New York Giants
February 3, 2002	New England Patriots	20–17	St. Louis Rams

January 26, 2003	Tampa Bay Buccaneers	48–21	Oakland Raiders
February 1, 2004	New England Patriots	32–29	Carolina Panthers
February 6, 2005	New England Patriots	24–21	Philadelphia Eagles
February 5, 2006	Pittsburgh Steelers	21–10	Seattle Seahawks
February 4, 2007	Indianapolis Colts	29–17	Chicago Bears
February 3, 2008	New York Giants	17–14	New England Patriots
February 1, 2009	Pittsburgh Steelers	27–23	Arizona Cardinals
February 7, 2010	New Orleans Saints	31–17	Indianapolis Colts

COLLEGE TEAMS PARTICIPATING IN THE BCS CHAMPIONSHIP GAME

Date	Champion	Score	Runner-up
January 4, 1999	1 Tennessee (SEC)	23-16	2 Florida State(ACC)
January 4, 2000	1 Florida State(ACC)	46-29	2 Virginia Tech(Big East)
January 3, 2001	1 Oklahoma(Big 12)	13-2	2 Florida State(ACC)
January 3, 2002	1 Miami (Florida) (Big East)	37-14	2 Nebraska (Big 12)
January 3, 2003	2 Ohio State(Big Ten)	31-24	1 Miami (Florida) (Big East)
January 4, 2004	2 LSU(SEC)	21-14	1 Oklahoma (Big 12)
January 4, 2005	1 USC(Pac-10)	55-19	2 Oklahoma (Big 12)
January 4, 2006	2 Texas(Big 12)	41-38	1 USC (Pac-10)
January 8, 2007	2 Florida(SEC)	41-14	1 Ohio State (Big Ten)
January 7, 2008	2 LSU(SEC)	38-24	1 Ohio State (Big Ten)
January 8, 2009	2 Florida(SEC)	24-14	1 Oklahoma (Big 12)
January 7, 2010	1 Alabama(SEC)	37-21	2 Texas (Big 12)

Observations:

1. There are thirty-two NFL teams aligned in eight

divisions. Seventeen of those thirty-two NFL teams have participated in the Super Bowl since 1999. All eight divisions of the NFL have had teams advance to the championship game.

2. There are 120 college football teams in the Football Bowl Subdivision (FBS) aligned in eleven conferences. Eleven of those 120 FBS teams have participated in the BCS championship game. Only six conferences have had teams selected to play in the championship game. You could argue that only five conferences have been represented because the schools that once represented the Big East Conference, Miami and Virginia Tech, are now in the Atlantic Coast Conference.

3. The list of NFL teams does not include rankings or recognize the division the teams played in. The media rarely mentions the division a NFL teams plays in or how a pro team is ranked; because rankings do not determine which teams advance to postseason play. I believe the ranking of college football teams is greatly influenced by conference membership. That is probably why a school's conference is important to college football fans.

4. In the list of BCS Championship game results you see both the school's conference and its ranking, either #1 or #2. Only six out of twelve years has the ranking been correct! The number two-ranked team proved to be better in half of the games. So if #2 was better than #1 half the time, could it be that the third ranked team could have

beaten second ranked team and been more deserving to play for a championship? Rankings are no way to set a playoff field.

5. A study of the scores of the two championship games reveals that the average margin of victory in the Super Bowl is 10.75 points. The average margin of victory in the BCS championship game is 14.83 points. A playoff designed to determine which two teams will participate in the championship game will create a better matchup than computer rankings or selection committees. The Super Bowl is far more popular with television viewers than the BCS championship game. The drama of a playoff generates the interest for the championship game as we see with the NCAA basketball tournament. The BCS system has two teams playing for the first time in a month on what seems to be a random weeknight.

★Intermedia
Publishing Group
Publishing That Works For You

Do you need a speaker?

Do you want Scott N. Galloway to speak to your group or event? Then contact Larry Davis at: **(623) 337-8710** or email: **ldavis@intermediapr.com** or use the contact form at: **www.intermediapr.com**.

Whether you want to purchase bulk copies of *It's Possible! Realignment And Playoffs - College Football's Opportunity* or buy another book for a friend, get it now at: **www.imprbooks.com**.

If you have a book that you would like to publish, contact Terry Whalin, Publisher, at Intermedia Publishing Group, (623) 337-8710 or email: twhalin@intermediapub.com or use the contact form at: www.intermediapub.com.